'Benjamin Hardy is one of the leading voices on well-being and productivity. *Willpower Doesn't Work* is an insightful guide to help us thrive in today's world.' — **Ariana Huff*** *rk Times* bestselling author, co-f***** **der and CEO of *Thrive Global***

'If you want to get more ****** — focus on motivation. Challengi***** **trol as a muscle, Benjamin Hardy***** ***productivity is really about clarity and commitment.' — **Adam Grant,** *New York Times* **bestselling author of *Originals* and *Give and Take***

'Change your environment, change your life. Ben Hardy's book is a prescription for excellence and contains the hidden keys to success.' — **Ryan Holiday, bestselling author of *The Obstacle Is the Way***

'In an age when few people think deeply about life, Benjamin Hardy is the exception. Read this book if you want to be better.' — **Jeff Goins, bestselling author of *The Art of Work***

'Uncommonly thoughtful: that's what I think of when I read Benjamin Hardy's work. Get this book and you'll better understand how to be who you truly want to be.' — **Jimmy Soni, editor of the** *Observer* **and author of *Rome's Last Citizen***

'Benjamin Hardy accomplishes something rare: the ability to blend practical actionable advice with a compelling voice. You're always better for having read something he's written.' — **Srinivas Rao, creator of** *The Unmistakable Creative* **and author of** *Unmistakable*

'Benjamin Hardy leaves you feeling inspired — like you have no choice but to commit to what you believe you should do.' — **Richie Norton, bestselling author of *The Power of Starting Something Stupid***

'I am fascinated by all things performance. Everything Benjamin Hardy writes challenges me to stretch a little further and dig a little deeper.' — **Joe Jacobi, Olympic Gold medallist and performance consultant**

WILLPOWER DOESN'T WORK

Discover the Hidden Keys

to Success

BENJAMIN HARDY, PhD

piatkus

PIATKUS

First published in the US in 2018 by Hachette Books, an imprint of
Hachette Book Group, Inc.
First published in Great Britain in 2018 by Piatkus
This paperback edition published in 2019 by Piatkus

1 3 5 7 9 10 8 6 4 2

A CIP catalogue record for this book
is available from the British Library.

ISBN 978-0-349-41794-3

Printed and bound in Great Britain by
Clays Ltd, Elcograf S.p.A.

Papers used by Piatkus are from well-managed forests
and other responsible sources.

MIX
Paper from
responsible sources
FSC® C104740

Piatkus
An imprint of
Little, Brown Book Group
Carmelite House
50 Victoria Embankment
London EC4Y 0DZ

An Hachette UK Company
www.hachette.co.uk

www.improvementzone.co.uk

CONTENTS

If we do not create and control our environment,
our environment creates and controls us.

—Dr. Marshall Goldsmith

WHY WILLPOWER DOESN'T WORK

Willpower doesn't work.

Let's be honest, you've tried to improve your life a million times—and a million times you've come back to the drawing board, frustrated. You've tried willpower to kick a bad habit but fell back into old patterns. You've tried New Year's resolutions, but by February, everything reverts back to how it was the year before. You've set big, life-changing goals but seem to find yourself far short of them despite hard work. After enough failure, it's easy to conclude that *you* are the problem. You must not have what it takes—the grit, the inner strength, the willpower. Perhaps you should just settle for the life you have...

But what if that assessment was all wrong?

What if the problem wasn't you at all?

Take the near-universal struggle to lose weight. A large portion of the global population is getting heavier despite exerting more and more effort to be thin. Billions are spent on fad diets and gym memberships—and for what? It is projected by several health experts that by 2025, more than 50 percent of all humans on planet Earth will be overweight or obese. Sadder still, those who are trying the hardest are struggling the most. There are a variety of explanations for this global crisis—for example, genetics, personality, a lack of willpower, or bad habits. But these aren't the cause of the obesity epidemic. Our radically changing environment is.

In the late 1800s and early 1900s, the world became industrialized, which drew masses of people away from farms and into cities. Rather than working outside as laborers, the trend over the last 100 years has been for people to work indoors, generally while sitting down. Rather than eating local food, most people eat food from a package.

Although the Industrial Revolution was a huge environmental shift, the information and technological age, beginning in the 1980s and 1990s, accelerated the changes to the now-global environment. Technological advancement is now moving at an exponentially faster rate, and very few human beings can adapt to the changes currently shaping our environment.

Most people are the casualties of these rapid environmental changes. Unequipped to properly govern themselves in a new world with new rules, many of them succumb to various addictions—primarily to technology, but also to stimulants such as caffeine, fast-absorbing foods containing high amounts of carbohydrates and sugar, and work.

All of these culturally accepted addictions fuel one another, putting people under constant stress and sleep deprivation. Put simply, most of us are in survival mode. To be addicted has become the norm, and if you want to control your life, willpower *should not* be your strategy of choice. There's too much in our environment that's pushing against us. Addiction expert Arnold M. Washton, PhD, has said, "Many people think that what the addict needs is willpower, but nothing could be further from the truth."

The key to getting out of survival mode and overcoming the cultural addictions is not to exert more willpower. Your willpower is gone. It was gone the moment you woke up and got sucked back into your smartphone. It was gone when you were bombarded by a thousand options and choices. White-knuckling your way to change doesn't work. It never did. Instead, you need to create and control your environment.

WILLPOWER DOESN'T WORK

Willpower, or the power to exert your free will against internal or external obstacles, has only recently bombarded the psychological world. But it has done so with force. According to the American Psychological Association's annual Stress in America Survey, a lack of willpower is frequently cited as people's top reason for not achieving their goals. Researchers across the globe are studying how people develop willpower and overcome willpower depletion. To be frank, willpower is for people who haven't decided what they actually want in their lives. If you're required to exert willpower to do something, there is an obvious internal conflict. You want to eat the cookie, but you also want to be healthy. You want to focus at work, but you also want to watch that YouTube video. You want to be present with your kids, but you can't stop looking at your phone.

According to psychological research, your willpower is like a muscle. It's a finite resource that depletes with use. As a result, by the end of your strenuous days, your willpower muscles are exhausted, and you're left to your naked and defenseless self—with zero control to stop the nighttime munchies and time wasters.

At least, that's what you've been taught.

Clearly, the research on willpower explains human behavior. But only on the surface level. The very fact that willpower is required comes from several fundamental sources:

- *You don't know what you want*, and are thus internally conflicted.
- Your desire (your *why*) for your goals isn't strong enough.
- You aren't invested in yourself and your dreams.
- Your environment opposes your goal.

Once these four principles are aligned within yourself, the internal debate is over. Thus, all future decisions regarding that matter have also been made. No questions.

So, are you serious about this?

Or are you just talking?

Are you still on the fence, or have you decided?

Until you decide, you'll be required to use willpower and will continue making minimal progress.

When it comes to achieving goals, making committed decisions involves:

- investing up front;
- making it public;
- setting a timeline;
- installing several forms of feedback/accountability; and
- removing or altering everything in your environment that opposes your commitment.

Rather than relying solely on your own internal resolve and strength, true commitment means you've built several *external defense* systems around your goals. It means you've created conditions to make the achievement of your goals inevitable. Everything has been put in place. You now have no choice but to act according to your highest desires. Too much is at stake if you don't.

YOU CAN DESIGN YOUR ENVIRONMENT TO PROPEL AND SUSTAIN SUCCESS

We adapt to our environments. Thus, a *conscious* personal evolution involves purposefully controlling and creating environments that shape us into the person we want to become. Everything in life is a natural and organic process. We adapt and evolve based on the environments we select.

You are who you are because of your environment.

Want to change? Then change your environment. Stop the willpower madness already.

These ideas run counter to a lot of self-help advice, which tends to focus on what *you* can do, by yourself and for yourself. The pervasive self-help advice is to focus on yourself. This makes sense, because we live in a highly individualistic culture. We've been conditioned to ignore context and obsess about ourselves.

Environmental design is different. It's about creating conditions that make your success inevitable. For example, if you want to be focused at work, you need to remove all distractions from your physical and digital workspace. If you want to eat healthy, remove all of the unhealthy foods from your house. If you want to get creative insights, get out of town and relax for a day or two. If you want to be more motivated, take on greater responsibility and increase the stakes for both success and failure.

Those who focus on environmental design recognize that a person's internal and external worlds are not clear-cut with fine lines. Although psychological research, for instance, distinguishes between intrinsic and extrinsic motivation, the reality is that the internal and external play off each other. When you change your environment, such as surrounding yourself with different people, your thoughts and emotions change. These inner changes then alter your values and aspirations, which requires you to further alter your external environment. Thus, it is by tweaking your conditions that you proactively shape who you become.

You design your worldview by proactively shaping your external inputs, such as the information you consume, the people you surround yourself with, the places you go, and the experiences you have. Most people, however, reactively and mindlessly respond to whatever environments they find themselves in, and thus develop a worldview leading to ineffective behavior and victimhood.

Which brings me to the very definition of "environment." In a strict sense, we all have internal, external, and interpersonal environments. However, for the sake of simplicity, in this book *environment* is that which is *external*, not internal. For example, your environment includes your physical surroundings, the people you choose to form relationships with, the information you let in, the foods you consume, and the music you listen to.

That which is external *shapes* that which is internal. Put more simply: Your worldview, beliefs, and values didn't come from within you, but from *outside of you*. If you grew up a white person in the southern United States during the 1950s, your worldview would likely have been shaped by that perspective. The same is true if you grew up in Europe during the Middle Ages, or in North Korea during the Communist rule, or in 2005 as a digital native with access to the Internet. Your goals, beliefs, and values are shaped by the cultural context in which you live.

Although the environment has never been more extreme

or more stressful, it is certainly *not* your enemy. In Western culture, particularly in psychological and self-improvement circles, the environment has been vilified. Perhaps the most common phrase among these groups is "to be a product of your choices, not your circumstances." At surface level, this is actually quite good advice. But it's also naïve and inaccurate.

Yes, your life is the product of your thoughts and choices, as many self-help books explain. But where do those thoughts and choices come from? They don't self-generate out of nowhere. You shape the garden of your mind by planting specific things from your environment, such as the books you read, experiences you have, and people you surround yourself with.

As will be shown, by shaping your environment directly, you'll be shaping your thoughts and behaviors indirectly. Furthermore, you'll create conditions allowing for desired behaviors which are not optional in common conditions. When you shape your environment, you'll have greater control over your thoughts and choices. Thus, instead of making the environment or "circumstances" your enemy, which has been the traditional advice of self-help, it's important to realize that your environment is actually *the only way* you as a person can truly change. New information, new relationships, and new experiences are how you change. You must gather and plant the right seeds from your environment to make a bounteous garden of your life. Consequently, although most environments will indeed shape a distracted and unfulfilled version of you, to attempt to be devoid of "environment" or "circumstance" altogether is not only impossible, but also foolish if you're seeking growth. Your environment can become your best friend. And as you'll see, you and your environment are one.

IF YOU DON'T SHAPE YOUR ENVIRONMENT, IT WILL SHAPE YOU

Unlike the common prescriptions of self-improvement— such as willpower and changing your attitude, which often are met against a negative and defeating environment—when you purposefully shape your environment, you can make quantum and radical leaps in your development. If you so choose, you can proactively place yourself into situations that demand ten times or a hundred times more than you've ever dealt with before.

How?

You adapt to your new environment.

Crafting highly demanding situations and then mindfully adapting to those situations is the key to success. Charles Darwin said, "It is not the strongest of the species that survives, not the most intelligent that survives. It is the one that is the most adaptable to change."

It's actually quite remarkable how quickly you can adapt from one environment to the next. Human beings are highly adaptive. For instance, Viktor Frankl reflected on his experience in a Nazi concentration camp sleeping *comfortably* next to nine other people on a small bed. Said Frankl in *Man's Search for Meaning*, "Yes, a person can get used to anything, just don't ask us how."

No matter how extensive the jump from one environment to the next—and, per Frankl, no matter how horrible the environment—a person can and will adapt. Rather than adapting to a negative environment, as the majority of the global population is doing, you can adapt to whatever environment you choose.

This book will teach you *how* to purposefully shape your environment. It will also explain *why* your environment shapes you. As such, a primary objective of this book is to show you that you can change in both small and extreme ways. You are not a fixed, independent, and unchanging being. Psychologically, intellectually, emotionally, and spiritually, your nurture is far superior to your "nature." And you are entirely responsible for your nurture; thus, you can guide who you become. Consequently, by the end of this book, you will be left with no excuses. You won't be able to point to your DNA, your past, or any of the other reasons why you believe you are stuck. Rather, you will understand the principles and be equipped with the strategies to create the environments that will ultimately create you.

WILLPOWER DOESN'T WORK

PART I

YOUR ENVIRONMENT SHAPES YOU

Chapter I

EVERY HERO IS THE PRODUCT OF A SITUATION

Understanding the Power of Surroundings

Historian Will Durant spent over four decades studying the history of the world and recording his findings in the eleven-volume masterpiece *The Story of Civilization*. He covered, well, the entire scope of human history. He looked at the great and defining moments, and more importantly, he studied the greatest and most impactful people the world has ever known.

And after those thousands of hours of study and careful reading, he concluded, somewhat surprisingly, that history isn't shaped by those giants. It isn't some clay that someone comes along and leaves their imprint on. No, in fact, what Durant concluded was that history was not shaped by great men, but rather by demanding *situations*.

Necessity, he found, is the single most important ingredient in the formula for greatness—not a particular individual's brilliance or a lone leader's vision.

This isn't easy for a lot of us to hear.

As a society, we tend to obsess about individuals and ignore the surrounding context that shapes them. Our movies highlight the charisma and talents of the kind of people who do amazing and impossible things. We believe in the hero's journey. We wonder whether their talent was genetic, or taught… or, in some cases, the result of performance-enhancing drugs. Our bookstores are filled with books proclaiming the individual characteristics we need to become superheroes ourselves: the aforementioned willpower, grit, self-esteem, and discipline.

In our individualistic cultures, we often believe our environment is separate and distinct from us. That somehow, someway, we are untouched by our environment. The truth is that you and your environment are two parts of the same whole. Who you are and what you can do in one situation is starkly different from who you are and what you can do in a different situation. Yet it is the Western way to isolate and decontextualize, whether it be variables in a science lab or ourselves. We're really good at putting things in boxes and missing the interplay *between* everything.

This individualistic worldview runs deep, and it's actually very difficult for us to consider otherwise or even comprehend that this might not be the whole story. Said psychologist Timothy Wilson, "People act the way they do because of their personality traits and attitudes, right? They return a lost wallet because they're honest, recycle their trash because they care about the environment, and pay $5 for a caramel brulée latte because they like expensive coffee drinks.... Often our behavior is shaped by subtle pressures around us, but we fail to recognize those pressures. Thus, we mistakenly believe that our behavior emanated from some inner disposition."

Unfortunately, the pervasive alternative to extreme individualism is complete determinism, where people are viewed as automatons with no individual will or agency of their own. The argument of this book is that *both* of these extremist views are misguided and dangerous. Without question, each person is shaped by their environment. However, each person also has great power in creating and controlling the environments that will ultimately shape them.

One interviewer pushed back on Durant's theory, the idea that environments are formative in the creations of greatness: "Haven't certain individuals, the genius, great man, or hero, as Carlisle believed, been the prime determinants of human history?"

It was Durant's response that supports the basis of this book:

"I think Carlisle was wrong... *the hero is a product of a situation* rather than the result being a product of the hero. *It is demand that brings out the exceptional qualities of man*... [Heroes] form the function of *meeting a situation which demands* all his potential abilities...I think the ability of the average man could be doubled if it were demanded, if the situation demanded."

THE POWER OF SURROUNDINGS

It's clear that this wasn't just the anecdotal speculation of a historian. Durant's insight that situations are what shape history (and people) have, in more recent times, been confirmed scientifically. Take, for example, the Equality of Opportunity Project, a groundbreaking study performed by Harvard economists Dr. Raj Chetty and Dr. Nathaniel Hendren. This project mapped the likelihood a person will improve their economic situation in the United States.

The results are devastatingly and shockingly clear: Your chances of improving your socioeconomic status are based very heavily on the state and even specific *county* within that state in which you live. In some counties, you have a fighting chance to improve your economic situation, while in others your chances are dim, nearly zero. Your specific environment of origin has a direct and measurable impact on the rest of your life, unless you actively change it.

Other studies have confirmed the widely quoted line from author and public speaker Jim Rohn that we are the "the average of the five people you spend the most time with." As it happens, we are also the average of the five people each of our five friends spends the most time with. For example, if your friend's friend gets fat, your chances of gaining unhealthy weight spike dramatically. This is called a *negative secondary connection*, and it's often more dangerous than a negative primary connection because you typically won't see it coming. In a more practical example: You aren't solely what you eat, but what you eat eats. Hence, the recent push to provide livestock with better and more organic nutrition.

A person's environment forms every aspect of their lives, from their income to their value system to their waistline to their hobbies. As will be shown throughout this book, *your potential is shaped by what surrounds you*. Every idea you have comes from what you've been exposed to. Who you become and what you do with your life are constrained by the people around you and the quality of information you consume. Garbage in, garbage out.

Or, as Durant saw it, you are either rising up or shrinking down from the demands of your situation. Most people are living small, not because they lack the inherent talent, but because their situation isn't demanding more of them. They haven't placed themselves in a position requiring them to become more than they currently are.

The good news is, it doesn't have to be this way.

MY STORY

The power of environment isn't just something I write about—it's something I study, experience, and marvel at in my everyday life. It is my core strategy for living and thriving. In August 2014, my wife, Lauren, and I moved to Clemson, South Carolina, where I attended graduate school in psychology. Initially, my interest was to study willpower in graduate school. However, throughout the course of my graduate studies, my research, and my personal experiences as a foster parent for over three years, my perspectives changed.

Delving deeper and deeper into psychology, and into my own human experience, I came to realize just how powerful the external environment is. This surprised me greatly, as I had been conditioned to downplay or even utterly ignore the environment around me. I assumed the environment was static and neutral and that people could autonomously do whatever they willed themselves to do.

Yet, in the course of my studies and life experience, I came to realize that context matters greatly—matters more than any of us are willing to concede. Immediately, I began to see just how much my own environment *had* shaped me. As many people do, I had gnarly and troubling experiences growing up. It wasn't until I left some of those places and experiences behind—and thrived as a result—that I realized my environment and I are two parts of the same whole. To change the one is to change the other. Thus, I came to realize I could quickly transform my identity, skills, emotions, and very worldview. My nature wasn't fixed. My environment, and thus my identity, were in large degree under my control.

Moving was one thing that helped me understand what our environment does to us. Another was becoming a foster parent. Our foster kids were born in a county that borders Clemson, where we lived. Their county is in the ninth percentile for upward income mobility—it's a very poor area with few jobs and fewer opportunities. Due to the legalities surrounding foster children, I cannot go into much detail about their early environment, but suffice it to say their home situation was far from ideal. The chances for these bright, intelligent, loving children to improve their lot in life, as well as their opportunities for happiness and fulfillment, if they had remained in their native environment were practically zero percent. But as Dr. Raj Chetty and Dr. Nathaniel Hendren stated, "The data shows we can do something about upward mobility...Every extra year of childhood spent in a better neighborhood seems to matter."

When we got our children, it was clear they came from a different world than we did. The five-year-old couldn't count to ten or identify the first letter in her name. The seven-year-old couldn't really read but fumbled his way through memorized words, some of them learned incorrectly. None of them could go to sleep on their own, and they all begged for medications to cure any physical or emotional concern.

To say it was a rough transition would be an understatement. Two completely different worlds clashed, and we were forced to become a new and cohesive unit. Lauren and I have been required to change immensely over the past three years as foster parents. We've had to learn parenting on the spot and patience beyond anything we'd ever mustered before. We've had to rearrange our lives, schedules, and priorities. Yet, this is exactly what we *wanted*, and we knew the demands of our new situation would *force us to evolve* into kinder, more loving people. We purposefully shaped an environment we knew would shape us.

Our children, and we along with them, transformed dramatically. They have thrived in their new, rigorous school. They are engaged in sports and other extracurricular activities. They've traveled to over thirty of the states in the United States in the past three years, greatly broadening their worldview and exposing them to different environments they never knew existed (and me, too, for that matter). They spent nearly twelve months over the past year refined-sugar free, which reframed their biology—including their self-confidence, ability to learn, sleep, and even be calm. They've averaged twelve hours of sleep every night since living in our home. We give them each nearly an hour of one-on-one help with writing, reading, and math each night.

People are often shocked how different our children have become. I say this not to brag about our parenting. We are far from optimal parents, but I will say we are better people for trying. However, I share this to highlight the radical change in environments we have all experienced, and how it has transformed them (and us) in the process.

My environment continues to compel me forward and to become the best version of myself I can be. My wife is such a lovely person. She makes beautiful and fun family videos. Recently, she made a video spanning the several years we've had our foster kids. It's crazy to see how small they were when we got them and how much we've all changed over the years. They were so cute, and such great kids. They've grown so much. It's amazing how memory works. I know, rewatching those moments, I have only fond memories, and my love for these kids grows every single day.

Watching those family videos Lauren has made humbles me to tears. I *love* these kids so much. They deserve the best

I can give them. They deserve a father who truly cares about them. They deserve a great life. They have become my inspiration and purpose (my "why") for succeeding as a writer. I want to make them proud. I want to be an incredible example to them. I want to provide the best possible life I can for them. My environment is a continual reminder of these things to me. I'm so grateful for that.

WHAT ABOUT FREE WILL?

It is crucial at this point to talk about free will and determinism. Some of us believe in free will (the concept that we can completely chart our own path in life), whereas others believe our lives as human beings are completely determined by outside forces, such as genetics. Both of these views are incorrect for several reasons. Complete "free" will doesn't exist. If it did, I could will myself to fly or make myself ten feet tall. Clearly, this isn't the case. There are external variables, like gravity, that *constrain* but do not fully determine my behavior.

On the opposite end of the spectrum, many have come to believe human beings are nothing but automatons who have no will or agency to direct their lives or make choices. Although our behaviors are shaped and guided by our circumstances, clearly there is a range of *possibilities* within each circumstance.

Even though you may be conditioned to act a certain way, you could do otherwise. Consider people who altruistically act in unexpected ways, putting their lives at risk to help others. When the stakes are high enough, any form of behavior is possible (as will be shown throughout this book). Thus, when you develop firm enough convictions or desire, you can choose to act contrary to your habits and conditions. You can choose to change the direction of your life by reshaping your surroundings. Even still, your possibilities are not infinite in number but are indeed constrained by your context.

Rather than complete free will or complete determinism, each person has a *contextual agency*. Put more directly, each person's possibilities for action are constrained by their context. As social psychologist Dr. Jeffrey Reber has explained, we live in "a physical world, with physical bodies and in homes with particular parents in particular cultural and geographical locations and temporal eras. We are not independent of these things, nor do they cause us to act, but they do constrain our choices." No two people have the same "free will" because no two people have the exact same context.

The truth is, we are never independent of context. For instance, are you free from gravity? Of course not. You're constrained, but not *caused* by gravity. What about air: Are you independent of air? (You better hope not.) People from the high regions of Peru are shorter than most of the world due to the thin air they breathe. The air creates certain constraints, but the people choose how they adapt to that. Are you independent of the cultural context in which you live and were born? Are you independent of the language you speak?

Some people may see these questions as pessimistic or limiting. They are not. They are realistic. Especially in a global world, we are more interdependent than ever. For example, I am writing this book on a laptop that I certainly didn't build, nor do I have the knowledge or skills to build it. I'm sitting at a table and on a chair I bought at Costco; I did not, nor would I want to, build either with my own hands. My body is filled with food I bought at a store, which required a great deal of effort and coordination in distributing. I'm reliant on my environment, and in many ways, I'm defined by it.

But here's the good news—I have a great deal of control over my environment. And so can you. Without the ability to change our environment, we *wouldn't* be able to change. To change one is to change the other. Harvard psychologist Ellen Langer has said, "Social psychologists argue that who we are at any one time depends mostly on the context in which we find ourselves. But who creates the context? The more mindful we are, the more we can create the contexts we are in…and believe in the possibility of change."

Thus, it's not free will *or* determinism. It's not choice *or* environments. Instead, it is choice *and* environment. More directly, it is the choice *of* environment. You are responsible for shaping and choosing the environments that will ultimately shape the person you become and the destiny you have. Environmental design is your greatest responsibility. Choosing and shaping your environment is at the center of what "free will" really means, because your choice of environment and external influences will directly reflect in the person you become.

THE NEW SCIENCE OF TRANSFORMATION

For a long time, psychologists believed there was a one-way relationship between the mind and body. Where the mind went, the body followed. However, recent research is showing that the relationship goes both ways. Yes, the mind can influence the body, but the body also influences and directs the mind. Consider the work of psychologist Dan Ariely, who explains a concept called "self-signaling" in his book *The (Honest) Truth About Dishonesty*. Self-signaling is the notion that we, as people, don't know ourselves as much as we'd like to think we do. In actuality, we judge ourselves and our character the same way other people judge us—by, as Ariely explains, "inferring who we are and what we're like *from our actions.*"

Your behavior doesn't come from your personality. Rather, your personality is shaped by your behavior. When you act a certain way, you then judge yourself based on your actions. Hence, you can quickly alter your identity simply by altering your behavior.

Purposefully acting in ways you know will influence your psychology is what psychologists call "precognition." The idea is quite simple: Something happens before, or "pre," the cognitive and emotional state. In other words, you can purposefully trigger, manipulate, and predict your inner experience through the use of specific behaviors. If you want to feel motivated, for example, all you need to do is clap your hands intensely for a few seconds, sprint around your house, and take a cold shower. Ask someone on a date, and regardless of the outcome, you'll see yourself as someone who takes risks. This shift in psychology will then alter future decisions.

Just as your body and mind have a two-way relationship, you and your environment also have a two-way relationship. When you change a part, you change the whole. Your environment largely triggers your mental and emotional state. Consequently, you can predict how you will feel in certain environments and around certain people. For example, when I'm in new and interesting places and surrounded by amazing people, I feel inspired and motivated. When I'm at a spiritual place, I am contemplative and often humbled. Precognition, then, is about *anticipating* and creating your future psychological state by shaping environmental factors in the present.

A friend of mine named Nate, who is a successful real estate agent, decided to try a personal experiment testing how his life would change by making a tweak to his environment. Despite making six figures, he's an extremely frugal guy. For years, he drove a beat-up Toyota Camry from the 1990s. The car ran great and the gas mileage was fantastic. But the car didn't create an environment of confidence in Nate's prospective clients.

His experiment was to upgrade his car and see how it affected his business. He spent over $110,000 on a decked-out Tesla. Four very interesting things happened within one month following his investment:

1. His online platform and presence grew rapidly as he shared about his Tesla and why he bought it. He got over

2,000 friend requests from people involved in real estate, people in his network.

2. The sales of his real estate education products quadrupled. This increase in sales allowed him to pay the car off just two months after the purchase. His environment now triggered immediate authority—which, according to psychological research, is a primary persuasion trigger.

3. With his new car, some of the biggest real estate investors and real estate education salespeople in his area began reaching out to him. He was now seen as "credible." Nate began getting invited to private events by his role models.

4. Nate's own psychology changed. Driving around in a nice car made him feel awesome. His confidence shot through the roof.

Nate's change in environment changed him—even if that change in environment was something as simple as investing in a more expensive car. His investment became a point of no return, heightening his commitment to his dream of becoming a successful real estate expert. By shaping his environment, he consciously created a self-fulfilling prophecy in real time. He created an environment that was now creating him.

Precognition was Nate's key to rapid transformation. He didn't know before buying the car the exact effects it would have, but he anticipated that his new environment would change him internally. Which is exactly what happened. Over a short period of time, Nate's identity and personality changed. Despite already being one of the top salesmen in his entire region, once he bought the Tesla, he quickly became *the* top salesman in his region.

Of course, not everyone is in a position to buy a Tesla. But this same principle can be applied in a myriad of ways. For example, by simply wearing different clothes, you'll feel different. If you want to feel more confident, dress better. Wear a little cologne or perfume. Do your hair differently. Small external tweaks have the power to create enormous internal shifts. You can then leverage these internal shifts to further alter your external environment for the better, thus creating a virtuous upward cycle of personal transformation.

NATURAL VERSUS DOMESTIC EVOLUTION

> Each species has been created with a tendency to vary, both under nature and under domestication.
> —Charles Darwin

According to Charles Darwin in *The Origin of Species*, evolution occurs in one of two ways, either naturally or domestically. Natural evolution, or evolution operating in nature, occurs as a species responds to the changes in the environment. Those who adapt best, win. This form of evolution is not preplanned and is largely unpredictable. Whatever changes happen in the environment are what lead to the changes in the species. Random evolution.

Domesticated evolution, on the other hand, occurs when

environmental factors are purposefully structured to yield specific "artificially selected" traits. Think precognition, but also prebiology, since both are shaped by environment. For example, people breed animals to have certain traits, such as speed, aesthetics, strength, or size. Domesticated animals and plants cultivated for food are generally far larger than their counterparts in nature.

Most people evolve the same way plants and animals do out in nature. They evolve in a random, unplanned, and unconscious manner. They *react* to whatever environment finds them. They haven't "begun with the end in mind" and worked backward.

The key difference, then, between how animals and humans evolve is that animals are the *direct* product of their environment, whereas humans are the *indirect* product of their environment. Although the environment is the medium through which all change occurs, human beings, if they so choose, can proactively *choose which environments they are in*.

One fact is certain: *You are evolving right this very minute.* Change is inevitable. Conversely, growth is optional and is rarely the case. If you don't pay attention to your environment, you will unwittingly become something you may not have wanted. Sometimes even your mindlessness can lead to your worst nightmares. I've seen this happen far too often. People tell me they want to "change their lives" or achieve "something huge," but continue spending lots of time stuck in their old habits or holding on to old buddies who are going nowhere in life.

My heart breaks for a specific high school friend, whom I'll call Matt. Just a few short years ago, he was in a beautiful marriage and well on his way to his dream job. Yet, he sabotaged and ultimately ruined both his marriage and his career prospects. Matt didn't realize the subtle influence *just one friend*, Eric, was having on him.

It turns out Matt was hanging out a few times per week with Eric. Together, they played video games, watched movies, and ate junk food. To Matt, a few hours per week "chilling" with Eric seemed *harmless*. Matt failed to realize he was slowly taking on the form of Eric's environment. Eric, though a friendly person, is also very cynical and negative toward life. He spends all of his free time playing video games. He's condescending and likes putting others down. Deep down, he hates himself, and thus finds joy pulling others down to his level.

During this time, I was busy working and doing my undergraduate degree. Yet, every six to eight months, I'd spend a few hours hanging out with Matt and Eric. During those short exchanges, I'd notice minor but recognizable differences in Matt. He was slightly more sarcastic or pessimistic. He'd make a negative side comment about his own wife. He'd periodically use swear words and derogatory language, which he never did before. The wallpaper on his smartphone was a pornographic image—one that his wife and young children could easily see. It's important to note that Matt's wife created an environment that allowed these behaviors to happen. Or more likely, she was reacting to the changes occurring outside of her and equally oblivious to their effect.

These changes weren't dramatic. In fact, they were a slow

boil, happening over the course of five years. But they weren't hard to see—especially to me, someone looking at Matt from the outside. I was able to see things in Matt that he couldn't see in himself. The changes occurring in him were minor when measured day to day, which is how we see ourselves. Yet, when measured in six-month intervals, the changes were quite stark. Accordingly, I could predict, even years in advance, that if he continued hanging out with Eric, he'd probably end up leaving his wife or smashing his life to pieces. To me, it felt inevitable.

The environment in which Matt purposefully put himself conflicted with him being a good husband and father. My private prediction indeed came true. Although sad, I was not in the least bit surprised. It's easy to predict where people are going in their lives. Your environment *reveals* you, both to yourself and to other people. Perhaps the clearest indicator of your internal identity is your external environment. If you are comfortable in certain environments, what does that say about *you*?

In retrospect, Matt would likely say that the changes he's made in his life over the past few years were of his conscious choosing. He wants to feel like he has ownership and control over his life. However, if you had asked him five years ago if he wanted to be divorced and jobless, he would have told you "absolutely not." He didn't plan for the evolution that occurred in him. He didn't realize his "friend" Eric was subtly and slyly chipping away at his value system and ambitions. He didn't realize that his environment had an agenda (as all environments do). Matt had surrounded himself with a loser, and then became a loser himself. To quote the Stoic philosopher Plutarch, "If you live with a lame man, you will learn to limp."

CONCLUSION: COMING-OF-AGE MOMENTS

In the movie *The Lion King*, Simba has a traumatic experience: His father is murdered. Simba is required to leave his home and joins Timon and Pumbaa, two outcasts who live a carefree life. Initially, Simba is repulsed by the rules Timon and Pumbaa live by. However, despite their low standards, Simba joins them and soon adapts to their lifestyle. He would have remained on this low-level trajectory, but a dire situation back home requires Simba to rise up and become a hero.

In order to take on a more powerful role, Simba is forced to face his past and deal with the emotions he's suppressed for years. He can't evolve without purging and letting go of all the emotional baggage keeping him in his low-level role and environment. If he doesn't rise to the challenge, the consequences will be terrible for the place and people he loves.

Simba had a coming-of-age moment, through which he became the person he needed to be. This was his point of no return. He was done living beneath his values and expectations. He was done lying to himself. He was done worrying about what people thought of him. He was willing to face all the consequences of his actions. He was willing to look and feel like an idiot. He was even willing to die for what he believed in. It became far more painful for Simba to continue running from the truth than running toward it. Consequently, he ran toward the truth and was empowered with a *why* that inspired power. He was then enabled to rise up to the role the situation required. He changed the environment and brought everything back in balance.

In a similar way, you need to have a full-on coming-of-age moment. This moment must also be a point of no return. Once you cross the point of no return, a great deal of confusion and ambiguity dissipates. You're no longer running from the roles required by your situation. You're no longer willing to allow yourself and those around you to needlessly suffer due to your lack of care. You're no longer concerned about the consequences or risks involved in being completely honest with yourself and everyone else. You're no longer willing to live a lie, and thus, you will no longer tolerate a mismatch between your convictions and your environment.

Being radically honest with who you need to be is all that matters now. The opinions of others are irrelevant. The uncertainties about the situation are irrelevant. The difficult emotions you must face are no longer barriers. Your relationship with toxic people can no longer remain the same. Either they must respect your situation and what you must do, or you'll have to leave them behind. There's no other option; the stakes are too high for you right now. There's no going back.

You're willing to face your fears and inner demons head-on. You're willing to give up your low living, your idleness, your wastefulness, your bad habits and addictions, your instant gratification, and your distractions. You're willing to take up the responsibility required of you. You're willing to be the person you must be. You're willing to change your environment for the betterment of yourself and those you love. It's time to be the person you know you can be. It's time to put cheap and small living behind you. Your world needs you to rise up. Your situation is poised.

Chapter 2

HOW YOUR ENVIRONMENT SHAPES YOU

The Myth of Willpower

According to Dr. Wendy Wood, a psychologist at the University of Southern California, throughout the better part of the twentieth century, scientists believed that if you wanted to change a person's behavior, the key was changing their goals and mind-sets. "The research was very much focused on trying to understand how to change people's attitudes," Wood said, "with the assumption that behavior change would just follow." The result was a plethora of scientific research and public health campaigns (and countless self-improvement books) about how to improve your attitudes and set better goals.

The result? A whole lot of nothing for most people.

Focusing on goal-setting and attitude only works for a small subset of behaviors, according to Dr. David Neal, a psychologist at Duke University. This small group of behaviors includes the ones you rarely perform, such as giving a public speech. The reason mental techniques and strategies focused directly on goal-setting are generally unsuccessful is because nearly all of your behaviors are outsourced by your environment. When you do something enough and in the same places, it becomes subconscious.

When you're first learning how to do something, such as driving a car, you are required to focus your conscious attention on your behavior and to exert a great deal of effort. You're required to think about each and every little detail, such as how hard or soft you push the gas pedal. However, eventually and after enough repetition, your behavior becomes subconscious, a process psychologists call "automaticity."

Although automaticity is essential to living and learning, it has its drawbacks. Most people have outsourced and automated their behavior to an environment that contradicts their desired goals. It is for this reason that New Year's resolutions and goal-setting rarely work. A person may want to stop smoking, but their environment triggers them to smoke at random and unexpected intervals. Willpower is expended and exhausted, and this person is left feeling like a loser.

However, when you outsource your behavior to a goal-enhancing environment, desired behavior becomes automatic and subconscious. Automaticity works in your favor. Once this is the case, your working memory is freed up to meditate and plan for other challenges. You no longer have to continually focus on your immediate surroundings. You're no longer fighting simply to maintain the status quo. Rather than paying rent and living day to day or moment to moment, you can invest in much bigger and better goals because your environment automates the behaviors that maintain your success and inner peace.

No wonder willpower has been placed under the media spotlight as essential to success. In a negative environment, willpower's all we have left. It's the life raft, the backup parachute. And we're depending on it to save our skins. It takes a lot of willpower to remain positive in a negative environment. It's difficult to constantly say no when those around you are eating junk food. Or even worse, when you're required to exert willpower in your own home because you bought junk food you knew deep down you didn't want to eat. This is a huge waste of mental and emotional resources.

Instead of being told to change their environment, the prominent self-help advice continues to charge people to change themselves. I can't emphasize enough how terrible this advice is. Throughout this chapter, I will use multiple strands of science and stories from history to show that it's actually *impossible* to change yourself without also changing your environment. Your environment and you are two indivisible parts of the same whole.

WHAT YOU CAN DO IS BASED ON ENVIRONMENT, NOT WILLPOWER

In 2014, Jasyn Roney became the youngest person to successfully land a backflip on a motorcycle. He was only ten years old. But what's even crazier than a ten-year-old doing a backflip on a motorcycle is the fact that backflips were considered impossible, even "video game material," back in the late 1980s and early '90s. But to Roney, doing backflips was just something motocross riders did. He grew up in a motocross culture where *everyone* did backflips. It was the norm.

The backflip became a reality back in 1998 when a motocross film spread like wildfire, showing people attempting backflips off a ramp into water. Suddenly, this unbelievable no-one-can-do-that thing began to look *possible* for the first time. In 2002, Caleb Wyatt became the first person to successfully backflip a motorcycle onto a dirt landing. This changed the rules of what was possible among motocross riders. By 2006, Travis Pastrana landed the first double backflip, and in 2015 Josh Sheehan landed the first triple backflip. This is evolution at work.

There is no doubt that the motocross riders in the '90s had willpower, passion, and a positive attitude. It was that the whole idea seemed physically impossible. No amount of willpower could create a backflip, let alone a triple backflip. The difference between ten-year-old Jasyn Roney and the legions of talented and daring motocross riders in the 1990s wasn't willpower or capability—it was context. When Roney was born, the backflip was commonplace. Raised and trained in that environment, he never thought to consider this once unbelievable act as impossible—he only had to think, "How can I learn to do one myself?"

And then he did.

EVERY ENVIRONMENT HAS RULES

Every environment has rules or norms. Those rules determine the behavior of the people in those environments because there are consequences to following and breaking those rules. For example, in some environments it's okay to smoke cigarettes while in other environments it is not. Screaming loudly is fine at a rock concert but not on an airplane. Wearing your shoes in some people's houses is acceptable but not in other people's houses. Driving on the left side of the road is correct in some places, while driving on the right side is correct in others. Every sport has rules, and those rules often change.

The rules in each environment can be both written or unwritten, spoken or unspoken. Whether explicit or implied, there are rules and they shape the behaviors and attitudes of the people within that environment. Take, for example, peer groups. Each group has norms that shape how the members think, act, and behave. It doesn't usually take a detailed explanation to discern the rules of a group of people. All you have to do is observe what they say, how they act, and how they relate to one another. You will know almost immediately if the rules of a particular group of people align or conflict with your own personal rules and norms.

Social norms are more powerful at controlling your behavior than your deepest ideologies and desires. For example, most people believe in being healthy and would love to be fit. Yet, despite these desires, they continue to purchase unhealthy foods. Most people want to be successful, but live in environments that facilitate consumerism and poor money habits.

A person's life, then, is not a reflection of their deepest-held values and beliefs. But instead, a person's life is a product of the social norms around them. If you remain in an environment conflicting with your personal rules, you have only two choices: Conform to a bad environment or battle it through willpower. Both of these are very poor options and ultimately lead to the same place.

EVERY ENVIRONMENT HAS A CAP

Consider the process of training fleas. A group of fleas is placed in a jar. Without the lid on the jar, the fleas can easily jump out as they please. However, with the lid in place, the rules of the environment are changed. Now jumping too high results in smashing into the lid, which doesn't feel so great. Consequently, the fleas adapt to the new rules and quickly become trained not to jump so high. Interestingly, when the lid is removed three days later, the fleas no longer jump out of the jar. A mental barrier had been formed into the collective consciousness, and the group of fleas now has a more constraining set of rules.

Not surprisingly, the new rules and social culture of the

fleas in the jar also influence the next generation of fleas, which go on to develop the same expectations for themselves as their parents had before them. The expectations of those around you establish your own personal rules and expectations. Psychologists call this the Pygmalion effect.

By remaining in immediate and constant proximity to their parents, the next generation of fleas can't transcend their environment. If, however, you were to take one flea out of that jar and place it in a bigger jar, surrounded by fleas jumping much higher, that flea would adapt. The old rules constraining that flea's behavior would be replaced with new rules. These new rules would not only alter the mental model of the flea, but also its genetic makeup.

This story of the fleas goes counter to the conventional understanding of biology and genetics but can be better understood in light of the new science of epigenetics. According to Dr. Bruce Lipton, a well-known biologist, "It used to be that we thought a mutant gene caused cancer," Lipton said, "but with epigenetics, all of that has changed." Lipton goes on to explain how his research revealed the science of epigenetics, and why a person's genes are not the sole cause of who that person becomes. As Lipton explains:

I placed one stem cell into a culture dish, and it divided every ten hours. After two weeks, there were thousands of cells in the dish, and they were all genetically identical, having been derived from the same parent cell. I divided the cell population and inoculated them in three different culture dishes...Next, I manipulated the culture medium—the cell's equivalent of the environment—in each dish.

What happened next was fascinating: by changing only the environment, these identical cells each expressed themselves differently. Says Lipton, "In one dish, the cells became bone, in another, muscle, and in the last dish, fat. *This demonstrated that the genes didn't determine the fate of the cells because they all had the exact same genes. The environment determined the fate of the cells, not the genetic pattern.* (Emphasis mine.) So if cells are in a healthy environment, they are healthy. If they're in an unhealthy environment, they get sick."

Put simply, epigenetics is showing that who a person becomes is based far more heavily on which genes are expressed than which genes are present. And gene expression is based in large part on environmental signals and choices. Thus, a person's biology is not fixed, but highly fluid and malleable. It's an exciting, and empowering, message.

YOUR VALUE IS RELATIVE, NOT ABSOLUTE

> Don't join an easy crowd; you won't grow. Go where the expectations and the demands to perform are high.
>
> —Jim Rohn

In some environments, you're a big fish in a small pond. In other environments, you're a small fish in a big pond. To change your environment is to change *you*. Take for example, a seventeen-year-old boy, whom I'll call Austin. His parents divorced when he was young, and he lives primarily with his mom. He spends every other weekend with his father. Although Austin doesn't realize it, when he's with his dad, he emotionally reverts to a much younger version of himself. According to Austin's mom, Austin becomes the five- to six-year-old Austin when he's with his dad. He becomes childish, immature, and seemingly uncontrollable.

The rules in his dad's environment are much different from the rules in his mom's environment. Furthermore, his role is different while with his father than while with his mother. Interestingly, when Austin returns home from his dad's house, he's established a routine that transitions him back into his mom's environment. Almost immediately when he gets home, Austin plays the piano for about thirty minutes. This behavior allows him to emotionally transition from one environment to another (precognition at work). It triggers him back into the role he normally plays, which is starkly different from the immature identity he acted out the previous three days.

Similar to Austin, who you are on Tuesday in one room is not the same as who you are on Wednesday in a different room. Around some people, you feel on top of the world. Around others, you can't think straight. You don't have an absolute value and unchanging identity. Like pieces on a chessboard, your value and capability are relative, not fixed and unchanging. The relationship *between* things (the context) is the reality, not the things themselves.

If you're close with some people, you could do brilliant and world-changing work. Among other people, you may be uninspired and dull, never fulfilling your deepest dreams (and, worse yet, never realizing what is missing in your life). Relating these ideas to the game of chess, former chess prodigy Josh Waitzkin explains in his book *The Art of Learning* (emphasis mine):

> While the intermediate player will learn how a Bishop's strength in the middle game depends on the central Pawn structure, a slightly more advanced player will just flash his or her mind across the board and take in the Bishop and the critical structural components. *The structure and the Bishop are one. Neither has any intrinsic value outside its relation to the other.* They are chunked together in the mind. This new integration of knowledge has a peculiar effect, because I began to realize that the initial maxims of each piece's value are far from ironclad. *The pieces gradually lose absolute identity.* I learn that Rooks and Bishops work more effectively together than Rooks and Knights. But Queens and Knights tend to have an advantage over Queens and Bishops. *Each piece's power is purely relational,* depending upon such variables as Pawn structure and surrounding forces. So now, when you see a Knight, *you see its potential in the context* of the Bishop a few squares away.

What Waitzkin described in terms of chess, I've seen and experienced myself, but to a heightened degree. A person's value is relative to their context, and unlike chess pieces, which can't change form, a person has the potential to change in powerful ways. Someone could go from a pawn, to a bishop, to a king, to something completely different.

During my undergraduate education, I worked as a research assistant to several professors. I thought I was pretty hot stuff. I worked hard, I knew the material, and I was sure that a bright future in academia lay ahead of me. After spending countless hours over two years doing research, I applied to graduate school...and was roundly rejected by all the schools I wanted to attend. Apparently, I wasn't as competitive as I was led to believe.

A few months after this humbling rejection, I met a young professor—Dr. Nate Lambert—from another department. Immediately, I saw something different about him. All of his research assistants were working on actual manuscripts. They weren't doing the common undergraduate labor but were being given far greater responsibility and professional training. I could see that working in Nate's research lab would provide far different possibilities than the labs I had worked in before.

My first day working with Nate, he gave me one of his old and unfinished research manuscripts to work on. "Get this baby polished up and we'll submit it for publication," he told me. I had never worked on a paper so close to publication, but given my new situation, my motivation was sky-high. I worked my brains out on that paper over the next week, and when I thought it was as polished as it could be, I sent it back to him. He liked what he saw and submitted it to a prominent journal, where it was eventually accepted for publication. "Wow," I thought to myself. "I just spent over two years with several professors and got nowhere near submitting anything for publication. Now, a week after meeting this guy, I already have a paper submitted."

I realized this was an environment that I wanted to be a part of—a productive, challenging, fruitful partnership. I was being pushed to excel in ways I hadn't in my other research relationships. I loved seeing my progress toward my goals. But even more, I loved seeing my skills, capabilities, and confidence grow while working with Nate.

My relationship with Nate turned into a very productive and life-changing mentorship. We became good friends and even accountability partners. Weekly, we'd go on walks and discuss the specifics of the papers I was working on. We talked about our big-picture dreams and goals, as well as our struggles. Nate gave me dozens of one-on-one coaching sessions, where he broke down weaknesses in my researching and writing skills. He eventually made me a team leader over a group of five other researchers. Four months after Nate and I met, we had over fifteen papers submitted to scientific journals. I was now poised to go to whatever graduate school I wanted.

Whatever writing and research skills I had in relation to Nate, they were nonexistent in the context of my other professors. I didn't know what I didn't know. And thus, I was unaware of the latent potential within me. Moreover, I was unaware of what true productivity could look like. My identity, abilities, and opportunities continue to be a reflection of my context.

The same is true of you.

You and your environment are extensions of each other. Who you are and what you can do in one environment is very different from who you are and what you can do in another. For example, you may be standing outside on a clear night and attempt to see Pluto with your naked eye. You could stand there for hours, weeks, years, even decades, and yet still you wouldn't be able to see Pluto. Willpower, a positive mind-set, and all the other things self-improvement guides have said you need wouldn't allow you to see Pluto with your naked eye. If, however, you used a high-quality telescope, the combination of you and that telescope would allow you to see Pluto.

Archimedes said, "Give me a lever long enough and a fulcrum on which to place it, and I shall move the world." Your environment is your lever. Archimedes didn't say he could move the world through grit and willpower. He humbly recognized his relationship with the tools in his environment. He and his environment are extensions of each other. Furthermore, Archimedes recognized that *a particular type* of lever was necessary to achieve his goal. Not all levers would provide him the leverage necessary to move the world.

Similarly, not all types of soil are sufficient to grow specific types of plants. If you want weeds, you will have many options of soil to choose from. However, if you want to grow tropical plants, you'll need a specific type of soil. It doesn't matter how much ambition or desire a certain plant may have to grow (or how much ambition you have to grow it!); if you don't have the right soil, it can't grow. The plant and the soil are both indispensable parts of the same goal.

YOU ARE ALWAYS ACTING IN A ROLE

Many people believe they have a fixed and unchanging "personality." That who they are at birth is, for the most part, who they'll be when they die. These people have bought into the notion that you and your environment are two very separate and disconnected things.

These people emphasize nature over nurture and fixate on what can't change rather than observing what does change. They "reify" themselves, which is to say, they believe that the most *real* part of them is untouched and uninfluenced by their environment.

This is the same logic as saying that a $1 bill and a quarter are *objectively and always* "money." Are colored pieces of paper and metal coins actually money? Or, as a society, have we created shared meanings about the value of particular coins and paper that we've created? Similarly, as a society, have we created shared meanings for things like "depression" and "intelligence" and "beauty" that we assume to be objectively real?

Is a quarter always a quarter?

Has it always been a quarter?

In the hands of a toddler, that quarter could be a plaything. In a different country, that quarter could be viewed as worthless. In a crucible of fire clay, that quarter could be melted down into a liquid. The quarter, depending on the context, is acting in a particular *role* based on who is holding it. Similarly, a person is never objectively depressed, intelligent, or beautiful. Rather, these are all subjective *meanings* based on

37

context. By overidentifying with any of these things, you put yourself in a box. You also make something that is subjective and fluid into something you believe to be objective, fixed, and unalterable.

Carol Dweck, a prominent Stanford psychologist, has found that people who believe their intelligence is fixed and unchanging have a very difficult time learning. The moment these people experience any form of difficulty or negative feedback, they mentally break and give up. Conversely, people who believe their intelligence is fluid and malleable are far more likely to grow and change. They are clay that can be transformed through experience, especially challenging and new experiences.

The belief that you cannot change leads to a victim mentality. If you are determined by nature to be what you are, then there is nothing you can do about your lot in life. Conversely, the belief that you can change leads you to take responsibility for your life. You may have been born with certain constraints, but you can change those constraints, allowing yourself to improve and grow.

Like the quarter, you are always acting *in a role*. The roles you play aren't your fixed and unchanging identity. Rather, you are *acting* a particular way based on the *rules* of the situation you are in. Like the chess pieces, your role is relative to what surrounds you. In some situations, you may play the role of a parent. In other situations, you may be a student, or a firefighter, or a friend, or, if you're playing with my six-year-old, you may be a trampoline to jump on.

A friend of mine, Blaine, works as a manager of an

industrial hose warehouse. Blaine told his friend Brad that he was just a "hoser," which disturbed Brad, who thought it belittled Blaine. Perhaps it would be better for Blaine to identify himself as a manager? Although it's common for us to overattach ourselves and to identify with the jobs we have, in reality, we are just acting in roles, whether that be a writer, a manager, a police officer, a lawyer, or a teacher. These roles quickly change as we change our context.

You've likely played roles that haven't been to your favor. For example, you may be an addict of some sort, perhaps an alcoholic. But you are not actually an "alcoholic." That would be reifying something about yourself that isn't actually you, but a role you are perpetually playing out in your life. More than who you are as a person, your addiction is a reflection of the environments and relationships you've allowed to be built around you. Addiction is a pattern, a subconscious outsourcing of behavior to self-defeating surroundings (much more on this later).

You can change your patterns. You can change your roles, but you can only do that by altering your environment—whether that means having frank conversations to reestablish boundaries and expectations, or whether that means physically separating yourself from certain individuals or places.

If you remain stuck in the same roles and patterns, it doesn't matter how much willpower you exert; your efforts will continue to be confined within the limiting context of your role. You'll remain hostage to a context that you mistakenly believe to be fixed identity.

But you absolutely *can* change your roles, even abruptly

and dramatically. People mistakenly believe they must be fully qualified to take on a particular role. But this is false. You actually become qualified *through the role itself.* For example, when Lauren and I became foster parents, we didn't have any parenting experience. Sure, I read several books on the topic, many with smart ideas and innovative solutions to try. But theory and experience are two radically different things. I imagine all first-time parents go through a similar trajectory— you learn through doing.

You can never fully prepare for anything in life. There's always a leap, whether big or small, from theory to practice. Rather than willpower, the leap into a new environment is instinctive, like a survival mechanism. Immediately, you'll go about adapting to a new role and new environment. So, instead of trying to prequalify to be someone, create the environment that will qualify you to become that person now.

SUMMARY

Individualism pervades self-help circles and content. As Dr. David Hawkins has said, "It is the illusion of individuality that is the origin of all suffering." Ironically, when you isolate things from their context, you put them in a box, which limits them from growth and transformation. Although this book recognizes constraints to personal growth, those constraints are less clear-cut and ironclad. Instead, a person's constraints are flexible and based on context. Rather than exerting more willpower and force, if you want to change your life, you simply change your environment and the roles you are playing. In order for you to successfully do this, you must realize that:

- what you can do is based on context, not willpower;
- every environment has rules;
- every environment has a cap;
- your value is relative, not absolute; and
- you are always acting in a role.

Chapter 3

TWO TYPES OF "ENRICHED" ENVIRONMENTS

High Stress and High Recovery

Courtney Reynolds is a young entrepreneur. She is intentional about how productive she is with her time. Consequently, she's *very* mindful of her environment. Around fifteen days per month, she lives in Denver with her business partner, Val. While in Denver, Courtney and Val commonly work eighteen-hour days. They are involved in several projects together. Their apartment has no distractions. There are no pictures on the walls. It's very simple. There are a few leather couches and plenty of open space to shoot videos for any marketing they need to do.

While Courtney is in Denver, she purposefully puts herself under a great deal of stress and pressure to succeed. There are always nearing deadlines, high expectations, and big promises to make good on. She gets an enormous amount done, but at a high price. Working so many projects and such long hours is mentally, emotionally, physically, and relationally exhausting. And that's exactly what she wants while she's in Denver. Her intention is progress and growth. Yet she knows the pace at which she works isn't sustainable. Consequently, she has a reset-and-recovery environment where she spends the other half of her month, in Las Vegas, Nevada.

Courtney's home in Vegas is designed to trigger intense relaxation, rejuvenation, and even joy. The walls are painted warm and inviting colors and are covered in beautiful art. The furniture and kitchenware are luxurious and inspiring. Moreover, Courtney is part of several social groups in Vegas that provide her leisure and deep connections. She often hosts people at her house. She sleeps ten to twelve hours regularly while she's there. She does have a small office in Vegas, which she uses a few short hours per day, mostly to just check in and manage her various projects. For the most part, she's entirely unplugged and recovering. You'll often find her running around town, dining in fancy restaurants, or taking part in many other entertaining activities throughout the city.

It's these regular recovery intervals that allow Courtney to push herself as hard as she does while she's in Denver. Proactive recovery is one of the secrets behind her incredible success at such a young age. Her strategic use of environmental design allows her to accomplish more in a month than many people do all year. When in Denver, her environment is optimized for productivity. Moreover, she herself is well rested, both physically and mentally, which enables her to push herself harder, longer, and deeper than most people.

Without even knowing it, Courtney has tapped in to some deep scientific understanding. She's structured what I'll call "enriched" environments, which allow her to be fully engaged in what she's doing. Human beings evolved needing two key types of environments: high stress and high recovery. In both of these environments, a person is completely absorbed in their situation. They are fully present and alive. In stressful environments, they're fully and 100 percent *on*. In recovery environments, they're completely *off*. Both these environments are enriching, fulfilling, and unfortunately rare.

The first type of "enriched" environment is by nature highly stressful: Call it *positive stress*, or *eustress*. But this is a very different type of stress than the common *dis*tress most people experience. Whereas distress leads to death and decay, eustress is the very thing needed for growth. Positive stress teaches us to test our limits and makes us stronger, accomplishing more than we ever thought possible. This is how Courtney lives half of her month, pushing herself often beyond her limits.

Which brings us to the second type of enriched environment: **rest and rejuvenation**. After stress, growth occurs in the state of rest. In order to become elite at anything, you need to continually shift from highly demanding environments to highly restful environments. In both instances, you need to be completely absorbed in each experience. While in a demanding situation, you'll need to rise to the occasion and focus. While in a recovery environment, you'll need to be completely detached from all the stresses of work, fitness, and the world in general.

In *The Adrenal Reset Diet*, authors Alan Christianson, NMD, and Sara Gottfried, MD, explain that unless we create the space to truly unplug, reset, refresh, and recharge, our body's natural and evolutionary response is to store fat rather than burn it. Elite health, creativity, productivity, relationships, and life require complete and regular recovery. This is how Courtney lives the other half of her month.

The science is compellingly clear about this. For instance, in fitness, the concept of "time-under-tension" explains that in order to grow and strengthen your muscles, you need to push them past their threshold. Running marathons isn't how you get healthy. Sprinting and recovering are. The deeper you push your muscles, the greater the potential for growth— but only if your recovery is equally long and deep. Actually, the recovery process should always be longer and deeper than the laborious process. Hence, sleep, prayer, vacation, leisure, fasting, and meditation (the keys to resetting and recovery) have never been more essential because the world has never been more demanding. Somewhere along the way, we've all forgotten this.

Similar to fitness, the best creative breakthroughs happen during mental recovery from rigorous and laborious work. For example, neuroscience has shown that only 16 percent of creative and mental breakthroughs happen while you're at work. Creativity comes from making distinct and useful connections. Those connections can't be made if you haven't thought intensely and pushed yourself deep into a project or problem, then rested. The mental and creative pearl won't happen while you're at your desk, but while you're resting. The best creative jewels are available only in environments far removed from the stresses and toil of your daily routine. Hence, vacation, travel, and complete unplugging have never been more needed than today. These need to be embedded in our regular life and routine, as Courtney has done. You may not be able to detach for a few weeks at a time, but you can unplug over the weekend.

Very few people take the time to recover from work, technology, people, food, and life. As a result, very few people have the energy and clarity to truly exert themselves in environments of extreme but healthy stress and demand. You need both types of enriched environments to thrive in your work, relationships, health, spirituality, and all other areas of life.

I recently met my friend Justin and his three kids at a local park. They were at the park because a friend of Justin's daughter had a soccer game. His daughter wanted to watch her friend play, and Justin was totally down to spend some quality time with his kids. I noticed that he didn't have his phone on him. He was completely with his kids, doing an activity that was important to *them*. It struck me that, at least in *that moment*, Justin was winning in life. He was living life on his own terms, according to his values. There was no fear of missing out. He was fully present with his kids, not semipresent while thinking about work or using his smartphone. He was with them. He was recovering and living life. No wonder he's so great at his job and in the other areas of his life.

THE NEXT EVOLUTION OF HIGH PERFORMANCE AND ACHIEVEMENT

It seems the "cutting edge" of self-improvement is based on psychological research of the 1960s, '70s, and '80s. Continuing to focus on mind-set, willpower, and goal-setting is an outdated and misplaced approach to success. It's not that these strategies are inherently bad. Rather, it's that the focus is entirely wrong. Most self-help guides put all of the pressure directly on the individual.

The next evolution of high performance and achievement takes the focus *off* the individual and places the environment at the forefront. Thus, ironically, the future of self-help will not be focused on "the self," but rather, it will be *focused on the environment* that shapes the self. At the core of this new thrust will be the installment of enriched environments.

While you're in an enriched environment, your desired behavior is automated and outsourced. You're fully present and absorbed in what you're doing, whether that's highly demanding work or rejuvenating recovery. Whatever you're doing, your environment has been proactively optimized to enable desired behavior.

Conversely, when you're in an ordinary environment, your desired behavior is not automated and outsourced. In most environments, you must remain conscious of what you're doing, and thus you must use willpower to act in desired ways. That's because most environments are optimized for distraction, not high performance or recovery.

The remainder of this book is focused on helping you

develop enriched environments so you can live on your terms and win at life, like my friend Justin, who enjoys fully present moments with his kids. Although it may seem counterintuitive, rest and recovery are actually the most important aspect of success. As Arianna Huffington has cleverly yet truthfully recommended, we "sleep our way to the top."

In today's highly demanding, nonstop, and overstimulating environment, taking the time to reset, rest, and recover has never been rarer yet more essential. Consequently, Part II of this book will teach you how to create enriched environments, optimized for rest and recovery. It is while resting that you'll get your most productive work done. You'll get your best ideas, have your most important moments with important people, and get clarity about what direction you should take your work and life.

Part III of this book will teach you how to create enriched environments, optimized for high stress and demand. A life of ease is not the pathway to growth and happiness. On the contrary, a life of ease is how you get stuck and confused in life. Although most people seek the path of least resistance and thus adapt to ease and idleness, immense challenge and difficulty should be your lot in life. Deep, not shallow, water is what you should want to swim. For example, trees that grow in windy and strenuous environments are forced to plant *deeper roots*, making them impenetrable to their difficult environment. You can't grow in life if you don't push yourself. To quote the poem by Douglas Malloch, "Good timber does not grow with ease, the stronger wind, the stronger trees."

The strength of a tree is dependent on the difficulty of

its environment. Good timber does not grow in easy environments. Neither do good people. If you want to get stronger, your workouts need to be difficult. If you want to become world class at what you do, your work needs to be better and more challenging. You need to have high expectations to succeed. You need to be tasked with projects beyond your current capacity, forcing you to plant deeper roots as a person.

PART II

HOW TO MAKE WILLPOWER IRRELEVANT

Chapter 4

RESET YOUR LIFE

Make Powerful Decisions Outside
Your Routine Environment

Tsh Oxenreider is a travel blogger who has spent the past few years traveling the world with her husband and three young kids. Before leaving the United States, completely unplugging from their lives, and traveling the world, Tsh was in a huge rut both in work and as a person. She struggled to find her purpose. She couldn't get herself to do the work she longed to do. She felt paralyzed.

However, once they left their routine and environment, she felt enlivened, inspired, and even motivated to work. It was as though the floodgates opened, and all sorts of ideas she could write about were pouring into her mind and soul. In her new and enriched environment optimized for recovery, she was making unique connections and was in a relaxed state. She was having new experiences and growing as a person.

It was while Tsh was traveling with her family, and completely removed from her regular routine, that she made some of the most powerful decisions of her life. She decided to make courses helping other people simplify and improve their lives. The reason Tsh was able to make this powerful decision is because she was having what psychologists call a "peak experience."

Abraham Maslow described peak experiences as, "rare, exciting, oceanic, deeply moving, exhilarating, elevating experiences that generate an advanced form of perceiving reality, and are even mystic and magical in their effect upon the experimenter." Maslow further argues that peak experiences are essential to becoming self-actualized as a person, wherein you have all of your base needs met and can fulfill your highest potential as a person.

Peak experiences are most likely to occur in enriched environments—specifically, environments optimized for rest and recovery. Hence, it is while you're traveling that you get your best creative insights. Consider the story of designer Stefan Sagmeister, who closes his New York studio every seven years for a yearlong sabbatical to rejuvenate and refresh his creative outlook. Sagmeister explains that during the one year away from work he comes up with his best ideas to pursue during the next few years. In a novel environment, and in a relaxed state, he's able to make unique connections in his brain. Moreover, he's able to truly assess what he wants with his life. What he's doing is seeking out peak experiences.

Peak experiences change the trajectory of a person's life and career. It is only by having powerful and paradigm-shifting experiences that you can truly see what's happening in your life for what it is. You can then make powerful decisions while in an elevated state to elevate your life and your standards for yourself. After seeing yourself and the world in a new way, you can transcend the petty fears and beliefs keeping you stuck in your present environment.

I've had several peak experiences and strive to have them regularly. Recently, I spent a weekend with my friend Richard Paul Evans, who founded a group for men called Tribe of Kyngs. The purpose of the group is to help men build genuine and intimate friendships (something that is rare today) and to provide an environment for men to overcome the challenges, have fun experiences, and raise their visions for their lives. A few weekends per year, Rick hosts a Tribe of Kyngs retreat at his ranch in southern Utah.

Rick recently invited me to check out his ranch and the retreat. I was blown away, first by how beautiful southern Utah is. Rick's ranch is right next to Zion National Park. But I was also blown away by the culture of the group and the purpose of the retreat. There wasn't a packed agenda of items to do. "Men are busy," Rick told me. "You need time to just relax. So there's no schedule for the next two days. Breakfast will be at nine a.m., but if you decide to sleep in, that's totally fine."

While at the retreat, I spent a lot of time riding four-wheelers and talking to the other men there. We even had a paintball gunfight. But I also spent a large portion of time by myself reading, writing in my journal, walking around listening to audiobooks, and viewing the beautiful landscape.

Interestingly, during this time away, my love and devotion to my wife, my kids, and my life back home insanely amplified. While outside of my routine, I could see the best parts of it for what they were, those parts that are so easy to accidently ignore and take for granted.

I didn't call my wife until I was at the airport, because a big purpose of the retreat was to unplug and reconnect with yourself and life. But when I did call her, I told her with more love than I had for a long time how much she meant to me. I'm ashamed to admit that I take her, our kids, and all the great things in my life for granted far too often.

But during this short ranch retreat, I didn't just get clarity about the great things already in my life. I also got lots of insights related to projects I'll work on in the future. The environment really matters, and Rick did a brilliant job creating an environment where I could have a lot of fun connecting to great men, and where I could just *really* relax, recover, reset, and reconnect with myself. I was able to think about what I want to do with the next few years. Because I was in a peak state, I visualized from my deeper soul and highest ambitions. I was high on life, and in that state was open to the brilliant ideas that entered my mind.

CREATING PEAK EXPERIENCES AND DOCUMENTING PLANS IN YOUR JOURNAL

According to Abraham Maslow, having a "peak experience" is rare. However, having peak experiences certainly doesn't have to be rare. Actually, having peak experiences, or putting yourself into a *peak state*, should be something you do on a daily basis.

The reason people consider peak experiences to be rare is because they haven't set up their lives to have them on a regular basis. Most people are very disconnected *from themselves*. They are living in an addictive and reactive state, triggered by a negative routine and environment. Even still, in those few moments when people purposefully pull themselves from their mesmerized state of unconsciousness, peak experiences can and *do* happen.

They are predictable.

You can create them.

What if you made being in a peak state a priority?

What if you literally needed to operate at peak levels on a daily basis in order to achieve your goals?

What if *that* was your standard?

Being in a peak state means you're operating at the level you want to be, so that you can achieve ambitions beyond anything you've done before. If you're not currently pursuing something you've never done before, you probably don't need to have regular peak experiences. But if you're in a state of growth, you'll need to position your life to have peak moments more frequently. Even more—you need to set your trajectory *from a peak state*. Because how you start something is generally how you finish it.

If you start right, you'll usually be able to stay right. But if you start wrong, it's very, very difficult to get things right. This doesn't mean you won't iterate along the way. It simply means that the power behind your initial decision will determine the trajectory. Most people make weak decisions from a non-peak state. Very few people, actually, truly make any real decisions at all.

Most people don't have enough conviction to truly make a decision. They aren't definitive. They aren't dead set. The stakes aren't high enough. Instead, they are like a ship without a sail. They go wherever life takes them. Theirs is a random and unconscious evolution. Their behaviors are reactive and without much consequence. It doesn't matter if they blow several hours roaming around on the Internet.

However, if you want to set a new path in your life, you need to make a powerful and definitive decision. And you want to be in a peak state while you make that decision.

How do you get into a peak state?

When it comes to having clarity about your life and goals, you need to give yourself a reset, regularly. The most successful people in the world purposefully carve out time in their regular schedules for unplugging, recharging, and resetting. Take the famous example of Bill Gates, who took "Think Weeks" where he would completely remove himself from work and all forms of communication. All he would do is think, learn, and rest. And he admits that his best ideas for Microsoft came during those rest and recovery weeks.

You may not have a full week to rest and recover. Instead, you could begin to schedule in "disconnected days," where you take a day off work and give yourself the full day to simply rest and recover. During that time, it would be helpful to leave your regular environment, and perhaps drive at least thirty minutes away to get adequate space.

During these disconnected days, you could spend a good amount of time thinking, relaxing, learning, and then writing in your journal. The reason you want to get out of your day-to-day routine and environment is so you can step out of the trees of your life and see the forest. You need some fresh air. You need to breathe and reset—just like fasting for your body—from the constant stress of going.

During these disconnected moments, it's best to remain fully present and unplugged from your work and life. This is very hard for most people, as most people are addicted to their technology and work. Hence, psychological research is finding the importance for psychologically detaching from work on a daily basis. Only those who truly detach—mentally, emotionally, and physically—can reattach when they start working again. In order to get absorbed and engaged in what you're doing, you need to rest and reset, regularly.

Rest is where you grow and recover so that you're empowered to get better and better at whatever it is you're doing when you're there. So you need to get away, even if for only a day. Get completely outside of your busy life and allow some time to reset and reconnect *to you*. A crucial component of this resetting is pulling out your journal and writing a lot. But before writing in your journal, you want to get your mind in the right place. That's why it is key to take at least thirty minutes to get out of your regular environment and prepare yourself mentally.

While preparing yourself, you may read or listen to some inspiring content. You may do a workout. Or talk to a close friend or family member who always seems to put you in an amazing mood. You want to put yourself into a peak state *before* you start writing. Naturally, being out of your regular environment will trigger positive emotions, especially if you know you're going to spend the next few hours diving deep into learning, recovery, planning, and visualization.

Other specific strategies to enhance your journaling experience are meditation and prayer. There is a great deal of confusion regarding what meditation is and what it's for. The mainstream belief, which stops so many people from developing meditative habits, is that meditation is about stopping your mind from thinking. This isn't what meditation is for. Meditation is for getting clear on what you want, and ultimately, about living a better life.

Meditation can take on many forms, as can prayer. To me, both go hand in hand. And giving yourself some time to pray and meditate just before you write in your journal puts you in an elevated mental state to write from. However, sometimes, that elevated state occurs after you start writing, especially while writing what you're grateful for. This whole process, the pre-journaling routine and the journaling process itself, is intended to take you deeper and higher into yourself, your dreams, and your ambitions.

Once you actually start writing, there are a few things that are helpful to focus your writing on: Start with gratitude and appreciation for everything happening in your life.

Take plenty of time to reflect on and write about all the details of your life and relationships.

Write about all the people who matter to you.

Write about how far you've come.

Write specifics about what is happening (and what has happened) since the last time you had a recovery session.

Recording your history is a crucial component of journal writing. It provides context to your ideas, goals, and plans.

Be radically honest with yourself about what's going on in your world while writing in your journal. After you've just expressed gratitude and appreciation for the brilliance (and struggles) in your life, you need to be honest with yourself about where you're not showing up.

While in a peak state, you need to commit to making specific changes. Write down the key changes you need to make to achieve your dreams and ideals. Write down everything that comes to mind. Journaling is a powerful therapeutic and healing tool. While writing about the things you need to change, openly write about the frustrations and difficulties that have led you to where you are. Write about why you've struggled to make these changes in the past.

Be very honest and vulnerable with yourself.

No one else is going to read what you're writing.

The purpose of this writing is for you to get clarity and to reestablish your priorities and focus.

If you can't be honest in your own journal, how can you expect to be honest in the rest of your life?

Write about your big-picture dreams. These could be framed as your life vision, your three- to five-year goals, or your goals for the next three to twelve months. It's good to take some time and think about what you're trying to do from the big picture before you zero in on the specifics right in front of you.

A key component of writing big-picture is that it reconnects you with your "why." It's very easy to lose sight of your why during your daily routine and busyness. Additionally, there is a huge difference between "means" goals and "ends" goals. And your ends goals are the things that truly matter to you. They are the things you want in and of themselves, not because they will enable you to do what you really want. For example, getting a college degree so you can get a great job is a means goal. But what is the end? The end is what really matters, and you can save a lot of trouble by beginning and continuing with the end in mind. You can avoid pursuing goals that are societal expectations.

It's good to have your phone with you, but only to act upon insights you get while writing in your journal, while listening/reading a book, or while pondering/reflecting. Often, you'll get insights about key people in your life. You should immediately make communication of some sort with the people who come to mind—whether that means sending them an email or text or giving them a phone call.

Recently while writing in my journal, I got the insight to send flowers to some people who have recently helped me. I immediately pulled out my phone and ordered flowers to their address. Then I continued my journaling.

WEEKLY PLANNING SESSIONS USING YOUR JOURNAL

It's effective to have a condensed or similar version of this recovery journaling session during a weekly planning session.

Every week, this is where you reflect on your previous week and make better plans for the following week.

Weekly planning sessions are essentially an expanded version of your morning journaling ritual, which will be detailed in the next chapter about staying on course. Specifically, in your weekly planning session—which should happen in your journal—you can write about the following things:

- How your previous week went (the good, the bad, etc.)
- What you did well (your "wins")
- What didn't go well (what you didn't do, who you didn't reach out to, where you fell short)
- Any significant events (like great moments with a friend, family, or a breakthrough in your work)
- What your plans are for the following week
- How you intend to take what you learned from your previous week and do better next week
- Your bigger-picture goals (in a short bullet-point list as a reminder of your "why" and "end" goals)
- Your proximal goals (things you're immediately working toward over the next one to six months)
- Specific to-dos you must finish the following week (including plans regarding your morning routine, learning, relationships, work, fitness, etc.)

As with the recovery journaling session, you should put yourself into a peak state before you start this planning session. The goal is to elevate your thinking, and then to make powerful plans and decisions from an elevated state. You want to reset your trajectory. Without making powerful decisions, how will you possibly create environments to facilitate those decisions? In order to consciously and proactively evolve, you need to commit to something specific. Otherwise, you'll reactively and randomly evolve based on whatever is happening outside of you.

SUMMARY

Lots of research has found that your best ideas won't happen while you're sitting at your desk working. Your brain operates best in a rested and relaxed state. Of course, you won't get brilliant ideas while resting if you haven't put lots of hard work and focus in while you are working. It's just like your physical body; it won't grow and get stronger while you sleep if you haven't pushed it to the limits while awake.

Additionally, your deepest insights will rarely happen in routine. While in routine, in your home, and regular environments, you're too laser focused on what's going on around you. You can't see the forest for the trees. Consequently, you need to regularly recover from life by getting away. Sometimes that will mean taking a break with your family. Sometimes that will mean taking a break from your family so you can eventually come back a better and more able version of yourself to love and support them.

Chapter 5

DESIGNATE A SACRED SPACE

Establish a Daily Environment to
Stay on Course

Once you make a decision, the universe con-
spires to make it happen.

—Ralph Waldo Emerson

Despite turbulence and other conditions keeping air-
planes off course 90 percent of flight time, most flights
arrive at the correct destination at the intended time.
The reason for this phenomenon is quite simple—through air
traffic control and the inertial guidance system, pilots are constantly course-correcting. When immediately addressed, these
course corrections are not hard to manage. When these course
corrections don't regularly happen, catastrophe can result.

In 1979, a passenger jet with 257 people on board left New Zealand for a sightseeing flight to Antarctica and back. However, the pilots were unaware that someone had altered the flight coordinates by a measly two degrees, putting them twenty-eight miles east of where they assumed to be. Approaching Antarctica, the pilots descended to give the passengers a view of the brilliant landscapes. Sadly, the incorrect coordinates had placed them directly in the path of the active volcano Mount Erebus. The snow on the volcano blended with the clouds above, deceiving the pilots into thinking they were flying above flat ground. When the instruments sounded a warning of the quickly rising ground, it was too late. The plane crashed into the volcano and everyone on board died.

An error of only a few degrees brought about an enormous tragedy. Small things—if not corrected—become big things, always. This flight is an analogy of our lives. Even seemingly inconsequential aspects of our lives can create ripples and waves of consequence—for better or worse.

How are you piloting your life?

What feedback are you receiving to correct your course?

How often do you check your guidance system?

Do you even have a guidance system?

Where is your destination?

When are you going to get there?

Are you currently off course?

How long have you been off course?

How would you know if you were on the right course?

How can you minimize the turbulence and other conditions distracting your path?

In the previous chapter, I explained how to disconnect and reset so you could set your trajectory. This chapter explains the importance of having a daily environment to ensure you stay on the right path toward your new goals. Moreover, you need a daily environment to re-create the peak state you had while you made your goals and decisions.

Just like an airplane, you need to continually make course corrections, or you will naturally go *way off course*. Daily, you need to ensure you're going the direction you want to. If you're truly committed to those changes, you'll need to prime yourself, daily, to be and act *from the position* of the new reality you're striving to create. As you do this, you'll be able to proactively shape situations and circumstances to make your goals happen.

WHY YOU NEED A MORNING ROUTINE

The core purpose for having a morning routine is to put yourself into a peak state in the morning—so you can then operate *from that state* for the rest of your day. Rather than being reactive, addicted, and unconscious in your morning, it's far better to proactively put yourself in a peak state in a ritualistic manner. Morning rituals are essential.

If you want to overcome an addiction—you need a morning ritual. If you want to be a prolific writer or creator—you need a morning ritual. If you want to be discerning, inspired, and present in your relationships on a daily basis—you need a morning ritual.

Why?

Because you need to trigger a state above your old and common ways of acting. If you want a different life, you must *be* a different person. Your morning ritual is what triggers a peak state. That state then reminds you of who you want to be and how you want to act. You then act from that state, as that person, for the remainder of your day.

If you want to change your trajectory in life, the two best places to do that are:

- Completely out of your routine and in an environment optimized for learning, growth, connection, rest, and recovery (see Chapter 10); and
- In the morning after a powerful and ritualized morning routine.

If you make a decision to live at a higher level, there will naturally be lots of resistance to your living out that decision. You have an environment built around you to keep things how they are. You have a mental model that matches your current life. If not so, your life would be different. Your confidence also matches your current life. If not so, your life would be different. So, when you make a definitive decision to live differently, you need to continually re-create the experience that spawned the decision. That experience— and its accompanying mind-set—needs to become your *new normal*.

So, you need to develop a routine of regularly getting yourself into a peak state. The best time to do that is immediately upon waking up. Because if you don't do it the moment you wake up, you'll immediately slip into your current state of operating, which is below the level of the decision you made while in a peak state. Thus, despite your best intentions, your behaviors will continue to match your current reality. You'll slip back into old patterns, your current reality will persist, and your dreams will remain dreams. You'll probably attempt willpower for a short time, but only to delay the inevitable.

If such is the case, then honestly, you should admit that the "decision" you made wasn't really a decision. It wasn't a decision because you didn't care enough about it to live it out on a daily basis. You didn't care enough about it to put yourself into that place. You didn't care enough to create a peak state, and then operate from that state on a daily basis.

You must first *be* a certain way, then *act* from that place, in order to *have* what you want. Be → Do → Have. Not the other way around. You need to act consistently from the peak state that formed your decision. It needs to become who you are. Being who you need to be becomes natural when you have a sacred environment and daily ritual for shifting yourself into the role and identity you want to make permanent.

YOUR MORNING JOURNAL RITUAL TO GET YOURSELF INTO A PEAK STATE, DAILY

Most people start their day in a reactive way. The first thing they do is look at their smartphone and immediately get sucked into a digital world of other people's information and agendas. They've set themselves up to live the remainder of their day in a distracted and reactive manner. Having a morning routine is important for a few key reasons:

- To reconnect deeply with yourself and your why
- To put yourself into a peak state, such that you can achieve the dreams and vision you're seeking in your life
- To frame yourself for what you really want to do that day
- To live proactively, not reactively, so that you avoid self-sabotage

A morning routine can entail many different things, such as fitness, meditation, prayer, working on a creative project, and so on. All of those things are incredible. However, the most essential aspect of your morning routine is writing in your journal. Writing in your journal is more powerful than simple meditation for the same reason that writing your goals down is more powerful than leaving them in your head.

Meditation and prayer are powerful ways to make your journaling session more effective. However, meditation, prayer, and visualization in and of themselves are not enough. You need to write down the insights, plans, and goals you have. And you need to write them down daily. Meditation, visualization, prayer, and journaling are all powerful activities that go very well together. But the journaling portion is where you solidify, clarify, affirm, and strategize your insights, goals, and plans.

Journaling makes the other keystone activities ten times or a hundred times more powerful. If you're not using your journal daily, then your meditation, visualization, and prayer will be far, far less effective. The key purpose of a morning routine is to put first things first. To focus on the important stuff in your life, rather than the urgent.

The goal is to put yourself into a peak state so you can then operate from that state in all you do, every single day. This is how you get out of survival mode and get massive momentum in your life. Momentum leads to confidence, which then leads to bigger and bigger dreams, better service and value you can provide, and a more congruent life. Thus, fitness and creative projects are great morning activities. However, nothing should come before priming yourself into the state of being you plan to operate from for that day. Here's where meditation and journaling come in.

Your conscious and subconscious mind, as well as your creative brain and energy levels, are in the optimal condition immediately following sleep. Writing in your journal first thing in the morning is essential for training your subconscious mind to achieve your goals. As Napoleon Hill wrote in *Think and Grow Rich*, "The subconscious mind will translate into its physical equivalent, by the most direct and practical method available." This morning journaling session only needs to be five to fifteen minutes.

When you write your goals and dreams down first thing every morning, you deepen your own sense of belief and desire in your goals. If you don't believe you can achieve your goals, you won't. If you don't really want to achieve a certain goal, it probably won't happen. So, every morning, you need to put yourself into a place where you're reminded of it, you believe it, and you want it badly. As a result, you'll work hard that day, and every day, to not be distracted nor derailed from what really matters to you.

It's also powerful to write your goals in an affirmative and definitive way. For example, if you want to make $100,000 or run a marathon, write:

- I'll be making $100,000 by [date]
- I'll run a marathon by [date]

Write your goals down daily. Then, in your morning mental state, you should write down everything you need to do to achieve your goal. This includes people you'll reach out to. It includes things you'll do this week, and even this day related to that thing.

CREATE A DAILY AND SACRED ENVIRONMENT FOR YOUR VISUALIZATION/JOURNALING

Some activities, such as visualizing and planning your future, making important decisions, or attempting to commune with the heavens, are most effective in a personally sacred environment. This doesn't mean you must go up to the mountains or to a temple, although both of those may be great options. Rather, you simply need a place that is personal to you, which triggers the mental state you need to think clearly.

My car is my daily sacred environment, but only when parked somewhere away from my house. Every morning, I get in my car and leave my home environment, with all its triggers and energy, and park either in a different neighborhood or even outside the gym before working out. I then spend between twenty and sixty minutes reading a good book, writing in my journal, praying, and meditating. Without fail, this daily act keeps me inspired and moving the direction in life I want to go. Aside from my daily sacred environment, a few times per month I drive a few hours to a personally meaningful place where I can completely shut out the world for a few hours.

Similarly, actor and comedian Jim Carrey applied this principle to create incredible opportunities. Despite growing up so poor that for a time his family lived in their Volkswagen van on a relative's lawn, Carrey believed in his future. Every day in the late 1980s, Carrey would drive atop a large hill that looked down over Los Angeles and visualize film directors valuing his work. That was his sacred place. He went up there every night. At the time, he was a broke and struggling young comic.

One night in 1990, while looking down on Los Angeles and dreaming of his future, Carrey wrote himself a check for $10 million and put in the notation line "for acting services rendered." He dated the check for Thanksgiving 1995 and stuck it in his wallet. He gave himself five years. And just before Thanksgiving of 1995, he got paid $10 million for *Dumb and Dumber*. The dream he created while in his sacred place became a reality. It became a reality because he continually reconnected with himself in his sacred place.

CONCLUSION

Do you have a sacred place you go to align and connect with yourself?

Do you have a place where you can meditate, think, pray, and visualize?

Is your daily journal the foundation for your long-term success?

Are you on track?

Do you give yourself the time?

Chapter 6

REMOVE EVERYTHING THAT CONFLICTS WITH YOUR DECISIONS

Subtraction is Productivity

Near the end of the movie *Interstellar*, Matthew McConaughey (Cooper) and Anne Hathaway (Brand) are trying to get themselves out of the atmosphere of a nearby black hole. However, there's a lot of gravitational pressure pulling them back. In order for them to escape, they needed to exert at least the same amount of pressure being exerted upon them by gravity. Newton's third law of motion states that for every action, there is an equal and opposite reaction.

The two astronauts formulate a plan. (Spoiler alert, if such a thing is truly necessary for a years-old movie!) They exert an extreme amount of effort using lots of rocket fuel from their ship's rockets. However, Cooper knows the energy from their rockets still isn't enough to get them out of the atmosphere. So he willingly sacrifices himself to save Brand. Once the rocket has enough momentum, Cooper detaches his part of this ship to lighten the load and propel the rest of the ship (carrying Brand) back to civilization. An action, and an equal and opposite reaction.

Newton's third law of motion isn't just a convenient Hollywood plot point—it's true (and effective) in your life too. Everything you have in your life is energy, and thus it creates an equal and opposite reaction. For example, if you have huge amounts of clothes overflowing from your closet, this costs you a large amount of physical space. But it also costs you mental and emotional space to sort through it all each morning to find an outfit, to move piles from one area to another, to think about the pieces that you know you should get rid of but you're not quite ready to let go yet...it all takes up more mental space than you think. And you're continually carrying all of that energy with you.

Beyond physical stuff like clothes, you are carrying a lot of suppressed emotions. Everyone is. And those emotions are very heavy to carry, making it almost impossible for you to evolve beyond your current atmosphere. Additionally, you are carrying relationships that, like gravity, keep you in your current environment. Newton's third law. The only way to get out of your current environment is to exert a force in equal and opposite proportion to all of the energy keeping you in your current atmosphere. That's a lot of force. Without question, you don't have the power or the energy to exert that level of force. It would be impossible to will your way out of your environment. The gravitational pull is seismic and gigantic.

Just as in *Interstellar*, the only way to effectively deal with Newton's third law of motion is to lighten the load. If you're willing to remove all of the excess energy keeping you in your current environment, it will take a far less equal and opposite force to get you out. There's really no way around it. You need to remove lots and lots from your life.

Although removing excess baggage from your life takes work, it's far more costly not to. Instead of doing a small amount of work for a lifetime of benefits, people avoid the small amount of work for a lifetime of pain and frustration. Gary B. Sabin, founder and CEO of several companies, tells a comical yet instructive story that illustrates how people needlessly make their lives harder because they avoid a little work.

Sabin had taken a group of Boy Scouts on a campout in the desert. The boys slept by a large fire they had made. In the morning when Sabin woke up and examined the campsite, he saw one of the Scouts who looked pretty rough around the edges. Sabin asked this Scout how he had slept. The young boy replied, "Not very well." When Sabin asked why, the boy said, "I was cold; the fire went out."

Sabin answered, "Well, fires do that. Wasn't your sleeping bag warm enough?"

The boy sat silently without responding. Then one of the other Scouts loudly volunteered, "He didn't use his sleeping bag."

Sabin asked the boy in disbelief, "Why not?"

Silence—then finally he sheepishly replied, "Well, I thought if I didn't unroll my sleeping bag, I wouldn't have to roll it up again."

This young boy painfully froze for hours because he didn't want to endure the torturous five minutes of rolling up his sleeping bag.

Don't be this kid. Don't spend your life—or even one night—in unnecessary pain. Do the work up front to lighten the shackles around your ankles. Remove the gravitational pull forcefully keeping you in an atmosphere you can't thrive in.

THERE WILL ALWAYS BE SOME DIFFICULTY WHEN YOU IMPROVE YOUR LIFE

Becoming a better person is difficult. You are where you are because of *who you are*. Your environment is a product of you. You're the magnet pulling in the patterns. If someone outside of you were to change your environment *for you*, you'd quickly find yourself in the same station you are now. Hence, most people who win the lottery quickly return to their poverty.

When a baby chick is trying to break out of its shell, it struggles. If you watch, you can feel terrible for the baby chick. You may even be tempted to help that chick by breaking its shell. But if you do this, you won't help the baby long-term. Actually, you'll probably kill the chick, because the very struggle of breaking out of the shell is what gives it strength to survive. Without the struggle, the bird wouldn't survive. It would remain weak and dependent. Similarly, you need to struggle if you're going to break out of your shell. The gravitational pull holding you down is the struggle you must learn to transcend.

It's not supposed to be easy to detach yourself from the life you currently have. You wouldn't be where you are if there weren't benefits. Acknowledge those benefits. Acknowledge that you enjoy being where you are. If you didn't, you would've changed your circumstances long ago. You're comfortable where you are. Consequently, it will be hard, at least emotionally, to get rid of many of the things that make up your current identity. This includes your physical possessions, your relationships, your distractions, your expectations, your excuses, and your story.

If you want to evolve to another level, you need to let go. There will likely be some withdrawals. You'll be tempted to revert back. But if you do, you won't make it out of your current atmosphere. You won't leave your current environment and enter into one with far greater possibilities.

ELIMINATE STUFF

The less you own, the more you have. Before you could possibly have a clear mind, you need to have a clear environment. Remove everything you don't regularly use. Start with your closet. Remove all the clothes you haven't worn in the past sixty days. You don't need more than six outfits.

Clean out your kitchen. Remove all the food you don't

really want to eat. If it's out of your environment, you won't think about it. If it is in your environment, you will eat it. Willpower doesn't work. You've lied to yourself about this flawed debate for years. Do it now. Go to your kitchen, grab a large garbage bag, and put all the food you don't want in the bag. If you feel so inclined, you can use two separate bags, one for garbage and the other to take to a homeless shelter. Whichever you prefer, get the stuff out of your environment immediately. You will feel amazing.

If you have a car, clean it out. Your car is meant to be a transport, not a garbage can and extra closet. Your physical space closely reflects your mental state. If your environment is disorganized, so is your mind. Everything is energy. Your environment is constantly influencing you whether you're aware of it or not.

If you have a garage, clean it out. Have a yard sale, send it to a thrift shop, or just throw it all away. Keep only what you need and actually value. Don't hoard stuff just because you have it. According to the sunk cost fallacy, people overly value stuff simply because they own it. Don't fall for this nonsense. Get organized. Clear the garden of your life. If you even have to waste five minutes per day on pointless garbage floating around in your environment, that's needless friction stopping you from achieving something you actually value.

At the most basic level, organization is about putting limits on things. In his book *Less Doing, More Living*, productivity and technology expert Ari Meisel says that in order to properly organize your life, you need to establish upper and lower limits on everything.

In his book, Meisel mentioned that if left unchecked, he's a technology hoarder. Before he organized his life, he had an entire closet full of power cables and other electronics. However, once he decided to reduce the gravitational pull in his life and eliminate the nonessentials, he established a limit of electronics he would have. He decided a shoe box was plenty. If he ever needed to add anything to the shoe box once full, he'd be required to take something else out and either throw it away or sell it. That box was *his limit* on electronics. Thus, that limit kept his electronics organized and tidy.

Here are a few more examples of limits you could potentially set to better organize your life:

- Never have more than fifty emails in your inbox.
- Never work more than forty hours per week.
- Never spend more than ten minutes per day on Facebook.
- Never spend more than $4,000 per month.
- Never eat out more than three times per week.

Upper limits are obvious. These are things you don't want to go over. But lower limits are also very helpful. These are baseline standards that you are fine going over. However, you don't want to go under these things. Examples of lower limits could include:

- I want to take at least one trip per month.
- I will run at least thirty miles per week.
- I will cook at home at least one time per week.

If you're serious about being organized, you should have limits set on nearly every aspect of your life. At the very least, you need limits set on your core priorities. Personally, because I embrace minimalism, I don't have to worry too much about putting limits on physical stuff. Every once in a while I clean out my closet and get rid of some shirts. Physically speaking, the one thing that gets out of hand for me is books. So I have to set a limit on the amount of physical books I have. Once I exceed that limit, I sell or give several away. For me, most of the limits I set revolve around *time*. Time spent working, time with kids, time spent meditating and praying, and how often I go on vacation. But it's just as vital when it comes to your physical environment. If your environment is cluttered, you'll have a messy mind. Everything is baggage that you have to carry.

For the best books on this subject, see Marie Kondo's *The Life-Changing Magic of Tidying Up: The Japanese Art of Decluttering and Organizing* and Greg McKeown's *Essentialism: The Disciplined Pursuit of Less.*

ELIMINATE DISTRACTIONS

Dopamine is a chemical in the brain that provides pleasure. It's intended to help us make correct choices. Unfortunately, in today's radically stimulating world, most people's dopamine levels are whacked out. Most people have become addicted to short-term dopamine boosts. Every environment is optimized for *something*, and most people's environment is laden with triggers that then prompt unconscious dopamine seeking. Their brains have become dependent. Their environment facilitates that dependence. It's a vicious cycle.

What does this look like in the real world? For most people, dopamine comes in the form of short-term distraction from what you should actually be doing. So, if you're working on a project at work and it starts to become difficult, or you start to get bored, what do you do? If you're like most people, rather than sitting with the struggle, you distract yourself. How? You probably check your email, or social media, or mindlessly surf the Web for a few minutes. You may grab some sugary sweet or processed carbs. Any and all of these activities provides a brief reward to the pleasure center of your brain. In other words, each of these activities releases dopamine.

Dopamine is the same chemical released when you take cocaine and other harmful drugs. It makes you *feel good* for a while. It's pleasurable. Unfortunately, that pleasure doesn't last. Just like the taste of a doughnut quickly fades only to leave you with long-term side effects, the short-term surge of dopamine quickly fades, leaving you wanting more. Like the sugar from a doughnut, the more dopamine you impulsively seek, the more your brain will develop a dependency on it.

If you have a smartphone, delete all the apps that aren't helping you become better at what you're trying to do. Just delete them. They aren't helping you. These are weeds cluttering the garden of your mind. Keep your cell phone away from your person as much as possible. Unless you need it while you're working, leave it in your car. When you are with your family, put it in your workbag. It will be there tomorrow when you need it.

Dopamine addiction and sensory pleasure seeking have become the primary American objective. What once used to be a country optimized for learning and sacrificing momentary pleasure for a better future, the overpowering message of today is to live for the moment. And that's exactly what people do. They live for this moment at the expense of going deep and pushing through distraction. Consequently, when something sucks, or becomes hard, most people anesthetize themselves with some distractive dopamine. Most people indulge themselves in momentary satisfaction at the expense of a better future.

ELIMINATE OPTIONS

The more choices you have, the fewer decisions you will make. In his book *The Paradox of Choice*, Dr. Barry Schwartz explains that having more options is not a good thing. Too many options leads to indecision and often half-committed choices. Because there are so many competing options, you're often left unsatisfied with a choice you've made. You're always left wondering if you made the right choice. Never fully committed and always looking back.

Michael Jordan has said, "Once I made a decision, I never thought about it again." This is confidence. This is self-trust. There's no fear of missing out. There's no questioning your own judgment. You know what you want and what you don't want. You recognize that with every choice you make, there are countless choices you could have made. Every choice involves opportunity cost. You can't have it all. And when you're committed to something specific, you're fine with that fact. You actually embrace that reality, because everything of true value comes with sacrifice. And you're fine with that sacrifice because you get the rare experience of achieving brilliant things, while most people are enjoying a large buffet of shallow decisions and empty commitments.

Consequently, the more options you can eliminate from your life, the better. This requires that you know what you want, or at least know the direction you're headed. Success isn't that difficult; it merely involves taking twenty steps in a singular direction. Most people take one step in twenty directions. Let go of vain and distracting pursuits you're not truly committed to.

Once you're committed to results, you make powerful decisions that remove or make easier all other decisions. For example, if you want to be healthy, simply remove all of the unhealthy food from your house. When we decided to make our home sugar-free, our kids hardly noticed. There was still food on the table and snacks in the fridge. Their willpower was unaffected because their environment took care of the decision. By eliminating bad options, willpower and working memory aren't taxed.

Although this may sound strange, you actually want to limit your future decisions. You want to create constraints around what you can do, because you know those constraints are your ultimate freedom. It takes wisdom to make choices you know will continue to serve you throughout the rest of your life. But in making those decisions, you know you'll be avoiding a lot of unneeded suffering and distraction that many people needlessly suffer through. As a simple example, I've made the decision to never drink alcohol. I don't look down on others who do. It was simply a decision I made that has *simplified* my life and continues to clarify my vision.

The fewer choices you have to make, the more powerful your choices will be. Eliminate all potential options that serve as nothing more than distractions. Embrace the opportunity cost. Let go of the fear of missing out. Go deep rather than shallow. Remove all internal conflict from your life. You'll be surprised how effectively a cleared-out garden can produce fruit. You'll also be surprised how peaceful it is to have created an environment that aligns with your highest values and aspirations. You'll be grateful for the strong person you were in the past, and for all the work you did to bring yourself to this point.

ELIMINATE PEOPLE

> Surround yourself with people who remind you
> more of your future than your past.
> —Dan Sullivan

People can either fill you with life or suck the life from you. American educator and university president Jeffrey Holland once told the story of a young man who for many years was treated poorly at school. Eventually, upon growing to maturity, he joined the army. While away from home, he had many successful experiences. He became a leader. He got well educated. He stepped away from his past and became someone new.

Then, after several years, he returned to the town of his youth. Although he was different, the same old mind-set that had existed before was still there, waiting for his return. To the people in his hometown, this young man was still the same guy he was before he left. They couldn't see the transformation that had taken place. Their paradigms were locked in place. And they continued living in the past, treating him as they had before. Sadly, this man readjusted back to his old ways. He came full circle: again inactive and unhappy. But this time, it was his own fault. He had chosen to surround himself with the very people who were holding him back in the first place.

One of my dearest friends calls me every three to six months to tell me, "Now is the time! I'm going to actually achieve my goals and turn my life around." What bums me out most is that this friend is completely sincere. She wants nothing more than to get out of the rut she's been in for more than a decade. She has huge dreams, ridiculous talent, and unmatched charisma. She's one of those people who could do anything she ever wanted. Success would come so easily. But it never happens.

She can't remove herself from the web of relationships that keep her stuck. She's surrounded by mediocrity and has become comfortable with it. So comfortable that it's become a self-made prison. All I have to do is ask when she last hung out with certain individuals to know she's nowhere nearer her dream than she was ten years ago. The real decision she needs to make is to *cut off* any relationships that contradict her goals.

Removing important people, such as friends and even family members, from your life can be very difficult. This doesn't mean you must permanently banish them, especially those you want to help and support; you just have to establish boundaries that keep you both from adapting negatively. The truth is, you'll never be able to force them to change. According to Strategic Coach founder Dan Sullivan, the best thing you can do is be a good example for them. And you can't be a good example by living below the level you believe you should.

ELIMINATE WORKING MEMORY

Working memory is your short-term memory. And it's very costly to try to keep things there. If you're trying to remember something for a finite period of time (minutes, days, months, etc.), you might end up forgetting. There's a *huge* opportunity cost to having a clogged and cluttered mind. Because you're fixated on holding the ideas you have in your head, you can't let your mind wander and get new insights. You can't ponder and reflect. It's like holding it way, way too long when you have to go pee. Don't do this to your mind. When you get insights or ideas, immediately record them. Get them down on paper or record them in audio. Outsource your thinking to your environment to free your working memory space.

Also, if you're like most people, there are certain types or patterns of communications you procrastinate. Often, this is more out of laziness than hostility. For example, I recently arranged to go to a movie with a friend a few weeks in advance. We got on each other's schedules and we were all set. I was stoked because I hadn't hung out with him in a while. Shortly after making those plans, I found out from Lauren that we'd be out of town that weekend.

Rather than immediately texting my friend, I waited a week. Because the movie was scheduled two weeks out, I figured I could tell him later. There was no urgency, so I procrastinated. I needlessly kept the thought in my head for a week: "You've got to tell Tyler you're not gonna be here for the movie." Had I just sent the text immediately, all would be resolved. The world would continue spinning, I'd have never thought about it again, and Tyler would have been able to better plan his weekend. If it takes less than two minutes, do it now.

Poor communication is one of the biggest roadblocks in having an organized and clear environment. Your life is the product of your standards. If you are willing to have unclear communication, that's exactly what you'll get in your relationships. But this obviously comes with heavy costs. A much better approach is to be respectful of the people in your life and respectful of your own working memory. Get into the habit of fast and straightforward communication when you have information others need. Don't procrastinate if you have a few days to send the communication. Get it out of your head now and allow the other person more time to deal with the information you give them.

SUMMARY

Elimination is the fastest path to progress and forward momentum. In order to transcend your current environment, you'll need to remove the excess baggage keeping you in your environment. It will take a little bit of work. But the payoff will far outweigh the cost. The key things to delete from your life include:

- Physical stuff;
- All distractions;
- Attractive but ultimately bad decisions;
- People who don't make sense;
- Commitments you never should have made; and
- Working memory.

Chapter 7

CHANGE YOUR DEFAULT OPTIONS

Make Positive Choices Automatic

I f you moved your silverware from one drawer to another in your kitchen, how long would it take to stop reaching for the old drawer?

Simply by changing the default option of certain choices is an easy way to immediately change behavior. People often take the first choice given them. Most default options that trigger unconscious behavior in most environments are far from structured optimally. In many cases, people are unknowingly performing at mediocre levels simply because that's how the environment was set up.

After deciding the university computer labs were wasting too much paper, Rutgers University simply made double-sided printing the default option on its lab printers. This small act saved 7,391,065 sheets of paper in the first semester, or roughly 1,280 trees for the academic year. Students, who frequently have no preference, are now required to manually select the option of printing only one side of the page. The option to conserve is made that much easier by becoming the default option.

What are your default behavioral options?

Nowadays, most people's default option is to distract themselves. At the end of the day, we grab some chips and turn on the TV. If you removed your TV and the chips, what would you do then? My wife and I have removed commercials from our lives (the average American spends four years of their lives watching commercials). We did this by unsubscribing from network television and using a Roku instead.

Here's the challenge with default behaviors: They are ingrained and triggered from the external environment. They are default for a reason, because they are unconscious and habitual. Because the environment prompts your behavior, it is the environment that needs to be disrupted.

ADDICTION COMES FROM HAVING INEFFECTIVE DEFAULTS IN PLACE

In the 1970s, Canadian psychologist Bruce K. Alexander was doing research on mice, trying to better understand the nature of addiction. He conducted several studies in which one rat was positioned in a small cage. Within that cage were two water bottles, one with regular water and one with water laced with either heroin or cocaine. Nearly 100 percent of the time, the rat became obsessed with the drugged water and drank until it died.

Dr. Alexander spent lots of time contemplating why this was happening. In 1978, he conducted a follow-up experiment that has since revolutionized the way drug addictions are understood. With funding from Simon Fraser University, Alexander and his colleagues built a large colony to house rats, with more than 200 times the floor space of a standard lab rat cage. This "Rat Park" experiment culminated in the leading breakthrough of the time: the underlying connection between a person's environment and addiction.

Within Rat Park, there were plenty of incredible things for a rat to do. There was lots of cheese, toys to play with, open space to run through, tubes to explore, and, most importantly, lots of other rats to hang out with. Also included in Rat Park were the two water bottles as used in previous experiments, one with regular water and the other with drug-laced water. Interestingly, in Rat Park, the rats hardly ever used the drug water, preferring the regular water instead. None of the rats ever used the drug water impulsively, and none of them ever overdosed, as the other rats did in the small and secluded cages.

This research on rats has been related to two similar instances among humans. First, the pervasive drug addictions that occurred among American troops during the Vietnam War. While overseas, nearly 20 percent of the 2.7 million soldiers developed an addiction to heroin. In response to this situation, President Richard Nixon announced that he was creating a whole new office—the Special Action Office of Drug Abuse Prevention—dedicated to fighting the evil of drugs. After laying out a program of prevention and rehabilitation, Nixon requested research be done on the addicted servicemen once they returned home.

The researcher charged with the job was a well-respected psychiatric researcher named Lee Robins, who was given extensive access to enlisted men in the army so that she could get the job done. First, she tested all the soldiers in Vietnam. Sure enough, nearly 20 percent of all the soldiers self-identified as addicts. Those who were addicted were required to stay in Vietnam until the heroin was out of their system. They were then monitored when they returned home to their lives in the United States. Yet, to Robins's surprise, only 5 percent of the previously addicted soldiers relapsed when they came home.

This didn't make scientific sense. According to the research, these men's brains should have been so wired and dependent on heroin that they'd have no choice but to impulsively relapse. People were outraged and questioned the validity or the research. Jerome Jaffe, the man appointed by Nixon to run the Special Action Office of Drug Abuse Prevention, said of Dr. Lee: "Everyone thought that somehow she was lying, or she did something wrong, or she was politically influenced. She spent months, if not years, trying to defend the integrity of the study." Being addicted in Vietnam didn't mean you were an addict in America.

Even though people couldn't fathom the soldiers' behavior, forty-five years later, Dr. Lee's findings are now widely accepted. Much of your behavior is unconsciously cued by your environment. Even behaviors you detest and don't want to engage in. For example, Dr. David Neal, a Duke University psychologist, said, "For a smoker the view of the entrance to their office building—which is a place that they go to smoke all the time—becomes a powerful mental cue to go and perform that behavior." The more repeated the cycle, the more ingrained the cue becomes, making it extremely difficult to resist. By changing the default of where the smoker parks their car and enters the building, they could eliminate the trigger.

Dr. Wendy Wood explains an important reason why triggers in our environment can be so powerful: "We don't feel sort of pushed by the environment," she says. "But, in fact, we're very integrated with it." Accordingly, both Neal and Wood suggest that the best way to alter addiction or any form of undesired behavior is to *disrupt* your environment. Even by making small changes, such as eating your impulsive midnight snack with your nondominant hand, can alter the action sequence and learned body response that is driving your behavior. This pulls your conscious mind back into the moment, allowing your prefrontal cortex the time to consider if you really want to make the decision you're about to make. Dr. Wood explains, "It's a brief sort of window of opportunity to think, 'Is this really what I want to do?'"

Hence, the primary theory behind why the Vietnam soldiers' relapse rate was so low was because, after being treated for their physical addiction in Vietnam, they returned to a place radically different from the environment where their addiction existed. Addictions, like behaviors, are environmental. In certain situations, the addiction was the default. In other situations, the addiction was not even a real option. Smokers, for example, can go hours *without even thinking about smoking* when they're engaged in certain activities or in certain situations. Most smokers admit to not experiencing smoking craving while on an airplane. Within that context, smoking simply isn't an option. Consequently, the craving doesn't persist, and the mind focuses on something else.

DESIGN YOUR DEFAULTS

You live in an addiction culture. Your environment is laden with trigger after trigger after trigger, such that if you don't take command of your environment, your default will be a wrecked life. The default for most people is to live in a reactive state—reacting to texts, emails, and other notifications. The current environment is simply too demanding, polarized, and invasive to ignore any longer. We are all addicted, dependent, and broken. Never have freedom and thriving been more available, and yet never have they been more inaccessible. To quote Peter Drucker, "In a few hundred years, when the history of our time will be written from a long-term perspective, it is likely that the most important event historians will see is not technology, not the Internet, not e-commerce. It is an unprecedented change in the human condition. For the first time—literally—substantial and rapidly growing numbers of people have choices. For the first time, they will have to manage themselves. And society is totally unprepared for it."

A self-improvement strategy that doesn't place the environment at the forefront is misled. Maybe it would work in another era when you didn't have the whole world at your fingertips. But the allurements are simply too potent now, the dopamine dependence too ingrained. Sadly, it seems most of the upcoming generation are set up to fail before they truly embark on their life. No generation has ever been tested with such tempting and chemically rewarding distractions. Unless the rising generation are hypervigilant about shaping their environment, there is little hope for them.

The most pervasive and addictive defaults in our culture revolve around technology, work, food, drugs, pornography, and people. You need to disrupt the triggers in your environment that lead to unconscious addictive behavior. You need to deepen the quality and intimacy of your relationships with other people. Our culture is being shaped to isolate us more and more from each other. Addiction is becoming an epidemic. When you have deep and meaningful relationships, your chances of unhealthy addiction are far less.

The following are four principles for overcoming harmful defaults in your environment.

PRINCIPLE #1: DON'T BE A SLAVE TO YOUR ENVIRONMENT

If you're like most people, technology operates you more than you operate it. Within the first few seconds of being awake, your technology taskmaster has you enslaved. Then, throughout your workday, you can't seem to focus for more than a few minutes without tapping into another dopamine hit via email, social media, or some other juicy Web distraction.

One study found that the average person checks their smartphone over eighty-five times per day and spends more than five hours browsing the Web and using apps. Hilariously, people check their phones more than twice as much as they think they do. For example, when was the last time you reached a stoplight without immediately looking at your phone? Put the phone in your glove box.

This lack of consciousness is reflected in all other areas of most people's lives—as we are holistic systems. No one component of your life can be viewed in isolation. If you spend several hours unconsciously using technology, how could you expect to be fully engaged in your work and relationships? Here are some of the outcomes of unhealthy smartphone use:

- Increased depression, anxiety, and "daytime dysfunction"
- Decreased sleep quality
- Decreased psychological and emotional well-being
- Decreased emotional intelligence
- Increased distress
- Decreased academic performance among students

One study found that if parents are reflective and thoughtful about smartphone use, their children are far more likely to develop a healthy relationship to technology as well.

Conversely, if parents are reactive and impulsive with their smartphones, how can they expect their kids to be any different? As with many things, parents are really good at telling their kids what to do, but bad at following their own advice. When it comes to learning, the primary method children use is observation and mimicking. Like the trained fleas in the jar, whose next generation was also stuck by the invisible barrier, parents' behavior becomes the standard for their children.

Other research found negative effects of using laptops and cell phones within one to two hours of going to sleep. Specifically, the study found that individuals who stopped staring at screens one to two hours before sleep experienced substantially higher sleep quality and less sleep "disturbances." The authors/researchers of the study concluded simply by saying "We should restrict the use of mobiles and laptops before sleep for sound mind and good health."

One day per week, you need to allow yourself to recover. Think of this as your own personal Sabbath, whatever your religious inclinations may be. Your day of rest. If you utilize this day of rest, you will undoubtedly have a far more engaged and effective week. Just like you should fully unplug from work every night, you should fully unplug your body from food and your brain from technology once per week.

Begin your technology intervention by taking a weekly fast, where you don't check your smartphone or get on the Internet at all for twenty-four hours. The purpose of the technology fast is to reconnect with yourself and your loved ones.

If you never give yourself a break from technology, it will wear you down mentally and physically. Although it may not feel like it, technology stresses your system. This continual stress puts your body in survival mode, making it store fat rather than burn it. Your smartphone addiction is making you fat. If you want to be mentally and physically healthy, you need to give yourself breaks. You need to reset and rest.

PRINCIPLE #2: WHEREVER YOU ARE, THAT'S WHERE YOU SHOULD BE

In our ever-connected culture, work–life balance has become a luxury of the past. In the 1930s, economists marveled at time-saving technologies and predicted that their grand-children (us) would be working only around twenty hours per week. They thought we would've developed technology and robots to do the majority of our work so we would have more free time to pursue enjoyable and meaningful activities. Not so. As it turns out, we are working more than we ever have before. And when we're not working, we're always connected.

The default, especially for millennials, is to *always be available*. This is not honorable, nor is it effective. Loads of research in the field of occupational health psychology is showing that in order to be fully engaged and effective at work, you need to learn how to psychologically detach from work. True psychological detachment occurs when you completely refrain from work-related activities and thoughts during nonwork time. This means you not only physically unplug from work, but you mentally and emotionally unplug as well. Research has found that people who psychologically detach from work experience the following:

- Less work-related fatigue and procrastination;
- Far greater engagement at work, which is defined as vigor, dedication, and absorption (i.e., "flow");
- Greater work–life balance, which directly relates to quality of life;
- Greater marital satisfaction; and
- Greater mental health.

If you don't properly detach from work, your chances of depression are much higher. Your relationships will suffer, as will your health. You are a system. Everything is connected. If you're radically imbalanced and unrested, how do you expect to be healthy, vibrant, and present? Because people are always connected, they remain in a state of continuous low-level stress. This stress is subconscious, but it ages the mind and body. In order to combat this weariness caused by not resting and resetting, people live on stimulants to keep them going.

The only way to psychologically detach from work is to change your defaults. You need to disrupt your work environment. Aside from putting healthy limits on your work and technology, you probably need to communicate to your colleagues that you will no longer be available during certain hours of the day. Rather than being upset, your colleagues will respect you more for respecting yourself.

Then you need to have a routine, or better yet, a *ritual* in place where you psychologically detach yourself from work. This is where you flip the mental switch of ON mode to OFF mode, so you can then go home and be present with your loved ones. This ritual should only be a minute or two at most. Before you leave work for the day (or, especially, for the weekend), write down what your top priorities are for the next day or week. When you write your thoughts down, your mind won't feel the need to linger on them or try to remember, because they've been written down and outsourced. If you need to send any final communications, do that. Finally, put your phone on airplane mode. This will serve as a powerful forcing function, triggering a flow state.

Beyond just putting your phone on airplane mode, either leave the phone in your workspace or put it away in a bag. This will serve as an additional forcing function, ensuring you don't get tempted to turn off airplane mode and just "check in." Hold yourself to a higher standard. Allow yourself to detach from work so you can fully engage with the rest of your life. Your work and everyone who may need you will be there when you get back tomorrow.

When writing this book, I frequently left my laptop at my office rather than bringing it home with me at night. This forced me to not mindlessly check in from time to time. If the laptop is home, the temptation is too great. Again, this is about making one decision that makes all future decisions either easier or irrelevant. It's making a decision and never thinking about it again. Set up the conditions that trigger flow and make living your highest values natural and inevitable.

If you commute home, you can listen to music or some educational material to unwind as you prepare to be with your loved ones. If you can't create boundaries for yourself and your work, then you'll never be fully effective. When you're in your focus mode at work, you should be completely unavailable except in case of serious emergency. Similarly, when you're home with your loved ones, you should be completely unavailable to your work and the outside world. As it relates to work, almost every "emergency" isn't really so. Almost everything can wait until morning.

When you allow yourself to be unavailable—physically, mentally, and emotionally—you'll live a far more present life. You'll experience a deep satisfaction actually being present with your loved ones. You'll be more attentive to their needs. You'll be more mindful and engaged. You'll be a better person in your relationships. Others will feel your love and affection more fully, since you'll be giving them your exclusive attention. Something they might not have experienced in a long time, if ever. To quote Dan Sullivan, "Wherever you are, make sure you're there."

PRINCIPLE #3: ACT ON INSTINCT AND INTUITION, NOT IMPULSE AND DEPENDENCE

What are your defaults in relation to food and addictive drugs, like caffeine? If you're like many people, you can't function without morning coffee. Caffeine in and of itself isn't bad. The problem is, caffeine has become people's default and dependence. It certainly doesn't need to be a default. You should be able to function well without it. It should be used with intention, not by compulsion. As a rule, you should act based on instinct, not impulse. Just because you could do something doesn't mean you do it. And when you do, it's because you want to, not because you have to.

According to research, one of the main reasons people use caffeine is because of the eight-hour workday. Caffeine has become an addiction based on an outdated cultural default. To be clear, a nine-to-five work schedule is not psychologically and physically ideal, especially now that most of us work with our minds and not our bodies. Mental work is far more taxing than physical labor. Despite weighing only three pounds, your brain sucks over 20 percent of your body's energy. You really have only four or five good hours of mental focus per day. If you work effectively, your work should take on the form of deliberate practice, where you're doing 90- to 120-minute power sessions, followed by 20 to 30 minutes of recovery in a different environment.

If you're going to use caffeine, technology, or anything for that matter, do it based on intuition and instinct, not based on impulse and addiction. This will require you to be mindful of your environment, as most environments (including cultural values around work) are now set up to trigger addiction and dependence.

PRINCIPLE #4: YOU NEED DEEP HUMAN CONNECTIONS TO OVERCOME ANY ADDICTION

The opposite of addiction is connection. Actually, addiction is the manifestation of having a lack of healthy human connections. Addiction is the product of isolation and loneliness, and it creates a downward spiral that creates even more isolation and loneliness. Addictions therapist Craig Nakken describes the inner psychology of having an addiction: "There is little in the person's life that is permanent and doesn't pertain to the addiction. The person has become totally afraid of intimacy and stays away from any sign of it. Addicts frequently believe others are the cause of their problems. They think people can't understand them. Thus, people are to be avoided...the aloneness and isolation create a center that is craving emotional connection with others...the Addict wants to be alone, but the Self is terribly afraid of being alone."

In the TED Talk "Everything You Think You Know about Addiction Is Wrong," Johann Hari explains that the way out of addiction is deep human connections. People need to believe their behavior matters, not only to themselves, but also to other people. Hari says in his TED Talk, "Because you can afford a ticket to the TED conference, you could afford to be drinking vodka for the next six months. But you're not going to do that. And the reason you're not going to do that is not because anybody is stopping you. It's because you've got bonds and connections you want to be present for. You have work you love, and people you love. You have healthy relationships...A core part of addiction, then, is not being able to bear being present in your life." When you don't have meaningful relationships, you desperately seek to fill that void somewhere else.

More than ever, our culture is more encouraging and accepting of addiction. In his book *Earth Making a Life on a Tough New Planet*, environmentalist Bill McKibben writes, "We've evolved a neighbor-less lifestyle; on average an American eats half as many meals with family and friends as she did fifty years ago. On average, we have half as many close friends." Despite being heavily connected through the Internet, people have never felt more alone. And in their lonely environment, the addictive cues have never been more powerful. Thus, people get caught in a destructive cycle, constantly seeking to bring their dopamine levels back to normal.

Unfortunately, when you've lost your confidence as a result of pleasure-seeking, it can be difficult to reach out and get social support. You'll probably try to convince yourself that you must first kick your addiction *before* you can reach out to people. After all, who would want to be in a relationship with you right now? As a result, you resort to willpower in attempts of clawing your way out of your addiction, all the while remaining isolated from the very people who could help you.

The classic movie portrayal of quicksand is incorrect. The heroine doesn't simply disappear, requiring a heroic dive after her. Real quicksand doesn't suck you in and swallow you up; it kills you with dehydration. The reason people die from quicksand is because they are alone, with no one to help pull them out. As they struggle to pull themselves out, each movement shifts them deeper into the sand until only their head remains. Thus, grand attempts with willpower actually get them more and more stuck. Willpower doesn't work. Neither does going it alone.

Just as you need someone else to pull you out of quicksand if you want to survive addiction, you need social support to pull you out of even seemingly harmless addictions like social media and caffeine. Any attempts at doing it alone through white-knuckling will only sink you deeper and deeper in.

A friend of mine recently checked herself into a six-month rehabilitation center. She made sure the environment was far away from her hometown, where her history, baggage, and triggers were. Quickly, she realized her new environment was optimized for making her face her dark side, the inner demons she had suppressed for years. The first month or two she was in treatment, her reaction was to withdraw herself from the group.

However, over time she came to realize that the only way out of addiction is by submitting yourself. Vulnerability is essential. Connection is the key, and it can be terrifying, especially when you've been as hurt as my friend has been. Joe Polish, who is both a marketing expert and an addiction expert, is a strong advocate for changing the cultural narrative around addiction. Rather than seeing addicts as bad people, it's important to see addiction for what it is: a solution. It's a solution for resolving pain.

Eventually, every addict, and really every person seeking permanent healing and transformation in their lives, needs to face the same bitter reality as my friend had to face. You can't overcome an addiction through willpower. You can't change your life on your own. You need other people. You need to learn to trust others. Transformation can only occur through collaboration, which requires two or more people. The whole becomes more than the sum of its parts. Rather than trying to "author" yourself, you give yourself wholly to another person and dedicate yourself to a cause you believe in. Said psychologist Viktor E. Frankl:

> True meaning in life is to be discovered in the world rather than within man or his own psyche. I have termed this constitutive characteristic "the self-transcendence of human existence." The more one forgets himself—by giving himself to a cause to serve or another person to love—the more human he is and the more he actualizes himself. What is called self-actualization is not an attainable aim at all, for the simple reason that the more one would strive for it, the more he would miss it. In other words, self-actualization is possible only as a side-effect of self-transcendence.

You don't need to be brilliant to have healthy relationships. You just need to be real and genuine. You need to be present and actually care about other people. This will require you to keep your cell phone off your body for large periods of time. It will also require you to be honest about your values, beliefs, and goals. If you can't be honest with others about who you are and who you want to be, your relationships will be shallow. You should surround yourself with people who love you enough to hold you to a high standard. Sometimes that means you'll let these people down. But if you can communicate honestly, people are very understanding.

There is absolutely nothing more important in life than other people. Nothing. Not even the brilliant and impactful work you will do. Especially with your spouse, children, immediate family, and close friends—those relationships are where your deepest joy and meaning can and should come. Those relationships are what drive you to be and do your best in life. They can serve as an incredible motivator. As for myself, my wife and three children are the reason I have purposefully shaped my life and environment the way I have. My primary goal in life is to provide well for them and to make them proud.

Chapter 8

CREATE TRIGGERS TO PREVENT SELF-SABOTAGE

Putting Failure-Planning to Work

An essential component of having enriched environments optimized for rest is outsourcing the need for willpower. However, you cannot control every environment. Sometimes, you'll be in situations where you'll be triggered to act against your desires and goals. Rather than relying on willpower, you'll need to create an automated response for how to deal with challenges. In other words, you'll need to create a trigger for the trigger. Once you get triggered to self-sabotage, that very trigger triggers you to do something more positive.

Sound complex? It's not. This is called *implementation intentions*, and it's a well-researched idea in organizational and motivation psychology. Once you've outsourced your proactive response to self-destruction to your environment, your level of rest and recovery deepens, because your level of internal consistency increases. At the most fundamental level, rest is about alignment and being in a state of peace and confidence. You can't have confidence if you continually act in ways contrary to your goals.

Here's how it works.

IMPLEMENTATION INTENTIONS

Implementation intentions come down to knowing ahead of time exactly what you'll do if you veer off course, as well as defining precisely what veering off course means for you. It's planning to fail so you can proactively respond. One way to apply implementation intentions is to predetermine the conditions in which you will quit working toward your goal. For instance, ultramarathon runners determine the scenario in which they will drop out of a race. They say, "*If* I completely lose my ability to see, *then* I'll stop." If they don't preset the conditions, they're likely to quit prematurely.

A mantra of the Navy SEALS is, *If it doesn't suck, we don't do it.* Unfortunately, when your mind fixates on how difficult something is, whether that's focusing at work or exercising, your chances of quitting skyrocket. The activity itself begins to feel impossible. Your brain seeks dopamine in whatever distractive form it can find. And, more often than not, you crack. Hence, you need to have implementation intentions in place. You do this by establishing an "if-then" response when you encounter tough conditions:

- If I'm tempted to check my email while working, then I'll get out of my seat and do twenty push-ups.
- If I enter the kitchen and am tempted to eat a Costco uncooked tortilla (so good), then I'll drink a big glass of water.

One of the main reasons these automated responses work is because they divert your attention from your triggered temptation. If you can distract yourself for even a few seconds, the craving often goes away. Furthermore, by following through with your plan and living in alignment with your goals, you'll get a boost of confidence—which is far more long-lasting than a shot of dopamine.

Research among children has found that imagining both the obstacles to their goals and their "if-then responses" improved students' grades, attendance, and in-class conduct. Additionally, and not surprisingly, separate studies have found that implementation intentions can strongly and consistently improve time management. Why? Because planning for the worst sets you up for reality. Rarely are the conditions perfect. And if you have a plan for what you'll do when things fall apart, you won't act in a reactive and unconscious manner. Instead, you'll confidently and consciously stick with your plan. You know why you set that plan in the first place, because you have goals that are worth way more to you than a short-term dopamine boost.

Other research has found that creating implementation intentions can increase your mental clarity regarding your goals. Having a plan—even one where you plan to fail—is motivating and clears the mental fog between you and your goals. Interestingly, this enhanced mental clarity can help you more mindfully realize when you're in a similar situation to one you've been in in the past. Thus, you can more readily and instinctively respond to negative cues in your environment, while minimizing false alarms.

The combination of enhanced mental clarity, boosted motivation, and a heightened sense of control is a potent cocktail against negative triggers and temptations. Perfection is certainly not the goal. But why not be proactive about living your highest values and intentions? Why become the unintentional product of a goal-conflicting environment? Why live a life of regret? If you're serious about living to the highest level, you need to plan for the worst and know exactly how you will respond.

PUTTING FAILURE-PLANNING TO WORK

Developing implementation intentions creates a strong mental link between the "if" component and the "then" component. The goal is for your "then" response to the critical situation to kick in automatically once cued. You'll want to practice your if-then response until it's a habitual trigger to the negative trigger. You can't just give in to your temptation and say, "Next time." You need to watch yourself do what you tell yourself you're going to do. This is not only how you develop habits, but it's also how you develop confidence and self-trust. Thus, you will have a preplanned strategy when you're at your worst, and you'll be far less likely to ever reach that point because you'll be a more confident person.

Your preplanned behavior should be initiated immediately, efficiently, and without need for further resolve or thought. It should be very simple and easy. Thus, your implementation is more than just a roadmap; it's an automated trigger—an external stimulus (a smell, a room, a person, a song, etc.) that sets off a trained reaction. And that means knowing what the circumstances of potential failure look like intimately—even viscerally.

My cousin Jesse was an avid smoker for over a decade, smoking several packs a day. Three years ago, he went cold turkey. Whenever he's feeling really stressed and craves a cigarette, he tells himself, "If I was a smoker, this is one of those times I would smoke." Then he continues on with whatever he was doing. An effective implementation intention can be as simple as a mental reminder. This trigger works for Jesse because it's very important to him that he no longer self-identifies as a smoker. And that deep commitment has helped Jesse train his brain to automatically remind himself in the moment he feels tempted to smoke.

My younger brother, Trevor, has a great strategy when he's triggered to play a video game to which he's addicted. The moment he's tempted or emotionally drawn to play, he pulls out his journal and acknowledges his feelings. He writes down that he was just triggered to play his game. He then does some stretching exercises for a few moments.

Without having this strategy in place, his default behavior would be to unconsciously respond to the cues in his environment. Unfortunately for him, a great number of cues in his current environment are now associated with his video game. So he's continually triggered to play. However, those environmental ties to his video games are becoming fewer and fewer as he reorients his automated response and replaces his addiction with something more beneficial. This is another reason implementation intentions are so crucial: You cannot actually overcome an addiction without replacing it with something else. The void must be filled. You must be strategic about filling that void.

VISUALIZE THE PROCESS, NOT JUST THE OUTCOME

Although writing down and visualizing the completion of your goal is extremely helpful, it's also essential to write down and visualize the process of achieving your goals. Research has found that by visualizing the process, which includes obstacles to your goals and how you'll deal with them, your performance will increase and your anxiety will decrease.

Want to give this a try? Pull out a piece of paper, grab a pen or pencil, and do this:

- Think about your top goal.
- Write down your top goal.
- Give it a timeline, preferably a fairly short one.
- Imagine all the potential obstacles you'll face in achieving that goal.
- Write those obstacles down.

- Now come up with an if-then response you will have to each of those obstacles.
- Write down your if-then responses to all of the obstacles you imagined.
- Write the conditions in which you will absolutely quit.

By first envisioning the various shapes failure might take, and then planning your automatic responses to each of those situations, you can start training your brain to put them into action long before you need to. There are a few important caveats to bear in mind, though. Obviously, if you're not very committed to a goal, your if-then response will likely be ineffective. Additionally, if you have low confidence in your ability to succeed, you probably won't—no matter how elaborate your plan.

Other research has found that specific if-then responses are far more effective than vague if-then responses. You'll set yourself up for success far more with something like, "If I walk into the kitchen and crave cookies, then..." as opposed to "Whenever I crave junk food, then..." Just like with visualization and goal-setting, the more specific your failure plan, the better you'll be at instituting it—and, hopefully, at staying on track to ultimately succeed.

CONCLUSION: HOW TO USE IMPLEMENTATION INTENTIONS

An essential component of environmental design is outsourcing your working or short-term memory to your environment.

You don't want to have to consciously think about your behaviors and choices. Instead, you want to create environments that organically foster the behavior you want. You want to create environments that either force the best out of you, or allow you to fully recover, reset, and reconnect.

Having worked with many addicts in my life, I've found that when a craving comes, there are a few torturous moments that will make or break you. If you can distract yourself for those few moments, the craving usually goes away. And because addiction is the opposite of connection, it's best to have someone you can immediately call when you get a craving. The worst thing you can do is rely on yourself. Being "independent" hasn't worked in the past. Rely on those you love. Your bonds and connections will save you.

Implementation intentions need not only be for momentary situations, but can also be more expansive. Quite frankly, sometimes you just get into a funk in life and need a reset. In such cases, you need some clear and automated strategies in place. Anything that is automated has been outsourced by the environment. You may have a place you go to contemplate, journal, hike, walk, run, or simply think when things have gotten out of control. Life gets out of control. I don't care how organized, smart, or great you are. From time to time, stuff falls apart and you lose sight of what's important and your connection with others and with yourself.

This is part of the process of life, but it doesn't need to be a negative thing. It can continually be a positive aspect of life if you have a system in place for dealing with it when it happens. Whenever I get into a deep personal funk, I have three close people I immediately call. These people are very different from each other, but have been key anchors during pivotal periods of my life.

After I've talked to each of these people, I pull out my journal and just start writing. Inevitably, I begin writing about my goals, the things I'm struggling with, and what matters most to me. Journaling is definitely one of the most powerful emotional regulation tools and for me serves as my daily therapy session. Writing with pen and paper slows the writing process down and allows my mind time to both focus closely and wander temporally. This act allows for inspiration to flow, especially because I spend a few minutes meditating and praying *before* I pull out my journal. I try to get into a mental space where my journaling will be inspiring and effective.

PART III

OUTSOURCE HIGH PERFORMANCE AND SUCCESS TO YOUR ENVIRONMENT

Chapter 9

EMBED "FORCING FUNCTIONS" INTO YOUR ENVIRONMENT

Make Change Happen

When you attribute the cause of something to yourself, rather than to your situation, you commit what psychologists call the *fundamental attribution error*. Since the 1960s, studies have confirmed, again and again, that even when people are fully aware that others are acting a certain way because of outside factors, they still attribute the behavior directly to the person.

Take politics, for example. If someone voted for a certain political party, you'd likely assume it's because that's just the type of person they are. You would downplay how their surroundings shaped that decision. Similarly, when someone cuts you off on the road, you're likely to immediately think they are an inconsiderate, thoughtless person, instead of wondering whether they were speeding home to pick up a sick child.

Psychologists are becoming keenly aware just how much external factors influence behavior. Rather than simply examining how a child's intelligence influences their test scores, for instance, researchers are now examining how "higher-level" variables also play a role in a child's test scores. These variables may include the size of the classroom, the quality of the teacher, a child's home life, the socioeconomic status of the child's family, what the weather is like that day, and many, many more.

The previous section explained in detail how your environment shapes every aspect of your life, from your goals and mind-sets, to your ability to perform and succeed. If success is your goal in life, then the next order of business is to determine which environments produce the best outcomes. Consequently, this chapter details the key components of "enriched" environments, which are circumstances that force you to perform at a high level. An inherent component of these environments is that they evoke eustress that creates focus and growth.

THE POWER OF SITUATIONS

Back in 1982, Tony Cavallo was working on the suspension of his 1964 Chevy Impala when his truck slipped off the jack and pinned him in the wheel well. In response to the loud noise, Tony's mother, Angela, dashed outside to see Tony trapped and unconscious under the truck. She began screaming for nearby neighbors to help, but in the state induced by the situation, she instinctively lifted the truck, which weighed thousands of pounds, off her son, high enough for some neighbors to rush in and place it back on the jacks. She then pulled Tony's body out from under the car.

Take the same scenario and change one variable: Imagine that Cavallo hadn't been pinned under the truck, screaming for his life. Imagine that he had called his mother out and asked her to lift the car. There's virtually no chance that she could've done it. But that situation summoned a deeper and more powerful side of her. That environment led to superhuman strength.

In the 1928 Stanley Cup finals game between the New York Rangers and Montreal Maroons, the starting goaltender for the Rangers, Lorne Chabot, got smacked in the eye with a puck and had to leave the game in the second period (helmets were not required until 1979). Unfortunately for the Rangers, it was uncommon at that time to have backup goalies. According to the rules of the game, in such situations the opposing team's coach must give permission for any substitutions. Although Alec Connell, a star goaltender who played for the Ottawa Senators, happened to be in the stands watching the game, the Maroons' coach, Eddie Gerard, refused to allow the substitution. After all, he wanted to win.

In an act of desperation, the Rangers convinced coach Lester to put the goalie gear on himself. Although Patrick had once been a great player, he had never played as goalie. At age forty-four, Patrick put on goalie pads for the first time and became the oldest player in history to play in the Stanley Cup.

From the stands came Odie Cleghorn, the then-coach of the Pittsburgh Pirates baseball team to stand in for Patrick as coach for the remainder of the game. The new and enriched situation required a different strategy. Their new game plan was to constantly check the puck at mid-ice toward the Maroons' net to keep it away from Patrick. Although not the best offensive strategy, they didn't want to take any chances. Amazingly, Patrick played out of his mind, saving nineteen shots and allowing only one goal. He didn't say, "I've never played goalie before, so I don't have the ability." He rose to the demands of his situation and the Rangers went on to win that game in overtime and eventually the entire Stanley Cup.

According to Dr. Martin Seligman, former president of the American Psychological Association, there are several psychological differences between pessimists and optimists. Most notably, pessimists are very quick to explain negative events as a permanent fixture of their identity. They (or life in general) are the problem, and there's nothing that can be done about it. Conversely, an optimist tends to explain negative events to themselves as *situational*, short-lived, and specific. When something goes wrong for an optimist, they focus on situational factors and strategize how they can change those factors in the future.

INTRODUCING FORCING FUNCTIONS

An effective way to optimize your environment is by structuring it with *forcing functions*, which are self-imposed situational factors that literally force you to act and achieve what you intend. For instance, when you intentionally leave your cell phone in your car when you get home from work, being present with your loved ones is outsourced by an enriched environment of rest and recovery. The act of leaving your cell phone outside your immediate proximity forces you to act as you intended. Besides which, it's simple: The phone isn't around. You can't use it if it's not there.

Forcing functions have this combination of usefulness and simplicity: You turn a behavior you'd like to do into something *you have to do*. It becomes your antidote to self-sabotage. Rather than relying on willpower, or lying to yourself that you won't mindlessly look at your cell phone while it sits in your pocket, you remove the option altogether. And that's the very definition of a forcing function. It's an embedded constraint that stops you from making certain errors.

Forcing functions are amazing because they are another way of freeing up your working memory. Rather than agonizing over what you should do or having to continually and consciously manage your behavior, you've created an environment that outsources desired behaviors. You can then be present in the moment and with your loved ones. You can focus on *their* needs because you're not constantly struggling with your own. You can be more mindful of the situations you are in, and thus have greater discernment into the needs of the present moment.

Forcing functions are about making one decision that makes all other decisions either easier or irrelevant. For example, my decision of removing all social media apps from my iPhone stops me from having to decide if I'll check my Twitter account every thirty minutes. Sometimes out of bad habit, I'll mindlessly pull out my phone to check Twitter and realize the app isn't there. I'm then reminded of the wise decision I made previously to shield myself from my own self-sabotage.

Keeping your options open often sets you up for paralysis and failure. It's better to purposefully remove options you already know may be pleasurable but ultimately distractive or even destructive. You can set up your whole life this way. And you'll have moments when you thank your prior self for making a powerful decision that is now influencing present experiences.

EXTERNAL DEFENSES FROM YOURSELF AND THE OUTSIDE WORLD

If you're serious about your goals, you won't leave it up to chance. Instead, you'll build several *external defense systems around your goal*. It's not about mind-set, willpower, attitude, self-esteem, or even discipline. On the contrary, true commitment is about outsourcing these inner strengths to an environment that makes them subconscious and instinctive.

One of my favorite examples comes from the entrepreneur Dan Martell. A few times per week, he takes his laptop to a coworking space or coffee shop and purposefully leaves his power cable at home. This gives him a few hours of battery life to get stuff done, which motivates him to work hard during those few hours. Martell also committed to his wife that he'd pick up their son every day from daycare at 4:30 p.m. Knowing his workday ends at four, he's far more aggressive and focused during his afternoons than he was when he gave himself endless amounts of time. Martell explains, "If you're serious, sometimes you need to go all in. Not because it's required, but more because it's what's going to set you up for the highest likelihood of a positive outcome. It's not about prioritizing or saying no, it's about setting up the right environment for YOU to be productive."

These strategically designed forcing functions serve as *flow triggers*, because they force you into the moment and what you're trying to do. Flow is the mental state where you're fully absorbed and immersed in an activity. While in flow, you feel energized, focused, and fully involved. Rather than being in a state of semi-distraction, as most people are when performing a task, flow only occurs when you're *completely in the moment*. Fully present. Your environment and your goals are at one. At this level of conscious awareness, time slows down, allowing you more cognitive control over your situation. The more flow triggers you can engineer into your environment, the more present you'll be and the better you'll perform.

PUTTING FORCING FUNCTIONS TO WORK IN ALL ASPECTS OF YOUR LIFE

The typical office job has very low expectations of its employees (even though it feels demanding). People are asked to do work—but they are rarely required to do things they've never done before. They aren't being forced into a role requiring a high level of responsibility and ownership. They aren't required to track and report their daily progress. If they fail to produce, the consequences are minor or nonexistent. The result is that people work with their cell phone next to their desk and with multiple tabs of distraction open on their Internet browser. Flow and deep engagement rarely if ever occur. They're distracted for most of their workday. And they're continually looking at the clock, waiting to go home.

In contrast, an enriched environment is almost exactly opposite from the normal conditions most people find themselves in. An enriched environment entails that you are fully engaged and present in the moment. Mental flow is the *normal state* in these types of environments, because the rules have been thus established. You create rich environments by altering the rules of the environment in the form of *forcing functions*. The most potent forcing functions include:

- high investment;
- social pressure;
- high consequence for poor performance;
- high difficulty; and
- novelty.

The more of these components you can engineer into your environment, the more enriched it will be. The richness of your environment can be measured by how regularly you are in a flow state while in that environment. If you engineer several forcing functions into your environment, flow will be your natural way of operating. As a result, you will perform at an extremely high level in everything you do.

HIGH INVESTMENT

In economics, there is a principle known as the *sunk cost fallacy*. The idea is that when you are invested and have ownership in something, you overvalue that thing. This leads people to continue on paths or pursuits that should clearly be abandoned. For example, people often remain in terrible relationships simply because they've invested a great deal of themselves into them. Or someone may continue pouring money into a business that is clearly a bad idea in the market. Sometimes, the smartest thing a person can do is quit. Although this is true, it has also become a tired and played-out argument.

Sunk cost doesn't always have to be a bad thing. Actually, you can leverage this human tendency to your benefit. Like someone invests a great deal of money in a personal trainer to ensure they follow through on their commitment, you, too, can invest a great deal up front to ensure you stay on the path you want to be on.

In 2002, with the rise of the health-conscious generation, Kelly Flatley decided to leave her job as a marketing coordinator to pursue selling the granola recipe she honed in college. After limited market testing with friends and family, she believed in her product, which didn't skimp on cheap ingredients, contained lots of healthy extras, and didn't include additives. But believing in her product was not enough. She had to make life-altering investments. Kelly invested her savings and time into renting a commercial kitchen where she hand-made her granola from about 8 p.m. to 2 a.m. each day. She called her product Bare Naked. After taking on a business partner, neither of them took a salary for the first two years. Kelly's dedication moved her from peddling granola at community events to selling the company only six years later to a subsidiary of Kellogg Company for $60 million.

Research has found that when you have a "growth" mindset, you are far more likely to persist when things aren't going well. You don't look at failures the same way most people do. Rather than as a negative, you view failures as feedback, something to learn from. Thus, highly committed and invested individuals with a growth mind-set are often viewed by others as ridiculous and risk-prone. With so much negative feedback and failure, the *logical* thing to do is quit. Yet, you continue to advance *not solely* because you are invested, but because internally you must continue forward. You don't care how many times you fail. You don't care what other people think about you. You are going to keep trying and trying until you succeed or can no longer keep trying.

How can you invest more of yourself and your resources into your goals as a forcing function?

SOCIAL PRESSURE

Tim Ferriss explains how after years of trying, he finally got himself to develop the habit of daily meditation. When he began a particular meditation practice that involved making sure he checked in with someone else about the practice, the social pressure forced him to develop the habit. He stated, "When you've told someone you would meditate two times between your next visit with them, you feel like an ass if you don't." It seems simple—but the lesson embedded in that story is powerful.

If you want to run a marathon, think of how you'd approach it if you used that strategy. You'd start with an up-front investment by registering for the race months in advance. You'd then publicly declare in person and via social media that you've signed up for a race. As psychological research has found, when you make a public commitment, you will feel a sense of social pressure to be consistent with what you've said. Additionally, you'll get multiple other people committed to running the race with you as well. You need people around you to be strong on days you feel weak. Thus, you will have at least one running partner in place, although more is better. Furthermore, you will track and report your progress to other people. You may even make it a competition with rewards and punishments. For instance, if you miss one of your runs, you'll be required to take your running mates out to a fancy dinner.

If you want to get a project done quickly, all you need to do is tell your boss (or whoever you report to) that you'll have it to them by a specific date. Make that date much sooner than you feel comfortable with. Sure, you may have a few late nights. But you'll never work harder in your life. Again, it's not willpower that's driving you, but external pressure, which pressure you've purposefully engineered because it forces you to achieve your goals.

What ways can you create social pressure to your current goals and projects?

HIGH CONSEQUENCE FOR POOR PERFORMANCE

> Courage can be developed. But it cannot be nurtured in an environment that eliminates all risks, all difficulty, all dangers. It takes considerable courage to work in an environment in which one is compensated according to one's performance. Most affluent people have courage. What evidence supports this statement? Most affluent people in America are either business owners or employees who are paid on an incentive basis.
>
> —Dr. Thomas Stanley

If you got fat the instant you ate ice cream, you certainly wouldn't eat it. If you got lung cancer the moment you smoked a cigarette, you definitely wouldn't smoke it. If your dreams were shattered the moment you scrolled your Facebook news feed, you probably wouldn't chill on Facebook so much. If your marriage ended the moment you entertained terrible thoughts about your spouse, you'd probably figure out how to transform your thinking.

When you're operating at a high level, however, the consequences for your actions are far more immediate. For example, if Michael Phelps started smoking and eating poorly, there would be an immediate drop in his performance. The reason is simple: He's operating at a very high level. Moreover, the consequences of failing at that level are also high. If Phelps coasts through a workout, or skips a training day, that might be the difference between a gold medal and not placing at all. When you're operating at a mediocre level, there is more room for mistakes and shortcuts—so people take them. You're not required to walk the razor's edge day in and day out. So why would you?

In order to perform at your highest level, your daily, hourly, and even minute-by-minute performance must mean something. Create consequences for failure—big ones. Not just social consequences, but consequences to the bottom line. Imagine yourself in a start-up and your funds are running low; you would focus accordingly. Imagine you're training for something big and can't afford to take a break. Bring other people into your goals and let that hold you accountable.

There's a lesson in that about the kinds of environments we can build for ourselves. If you have high standards for yourself, and you're surrounded by people who hold you to a high standard, then *it's expected* you'll perform well. If you don't do your job, then everything is put into jeopardy. Because when you're at the highest level, things need to be running efficiently, or they become average like everything else. Thus, you need to be highly accountable to yourself and those who rely on you at this level.

Take a look at your current situation. What are the consequences if you don't perform at your highest level?

What ways can you make the consequences of your actions more salient and motivating?

HIGH DIFFICULTY

> Rugged and hostile environments teach us. And
> they teach us by leveraging real fear.
>
> —Michael Gervais

In a story told by educator and religious leader Dr. David Bednar, a young man had recently purchased a pickup truck. Needing some firewood, he thought it a great opportunity to test his new truck. After driving up the snowy mountains and out of cell phone range, he found a spot to park near some trees. He pulled off the road to park and got stuck in deep snow. Desperate, he tried everything he could to get out. When he switched from reverse to drive and spun out his tires, his truck got stuck deeper and deeper. He put twigs under the stuck tire in hopes they would provide traction, but to no avail. He used a shovel and tried digging around the tire, but he was stuck too deep.

Eventually, he became incredibly discouraged. The sun was hastily descending and the weather getting bitterly cold.

He wasn't sure what to do. He offered a simple prayer and got the urge to start cutting wood. He worked for a few hours, chopping down trees and putting large pieces into the back of his truck. Once the truck was full, he hopped in and turned it on. After a moment of humble silence, he tried reversing out. The heavy load of wood provided the needed traction to get out of the snow, to get back onto the road, and to move forward. Without the load of wood in his truck, he would have remained stuck.

Most people mistakenly believe that happiness is the absence of a load. We want life to be easy, without challenge or difficulty. However, it is by having a load that we can have the traction needed to move forward in our lives. Our shoulders grow to bear the weight on them. When we don't carry a substantial weight of personal responsibility, we can quickly become stuck like the man's truck in the snow.

I've seen this come true in my own life. It wasn't until after I became a foster parent—a substantial load indeed—that I was able to get the traction needed to develop my career as a writer. Before having that personal load to carry, I was somewhat complacent. I lacked urgency. Despite wanting deeply to become a writer, I didn't have the traction to move forward. My situation wasn't forcing me to succeed and the stakes weren't high enough. I had plenty of leeway and figured I'd get around to it at some point.

NOVELTY

When you do things you've never done before, you're naturally more focused and engaged. When exposed to new information, your brain is required to work much harder. You're connecting new things into your existing mental model, thus rewriting the chemistry of your brain. This not only keeps you focused, but it also transforms you as a person. It keeps you alive and growing, rather than stale and decaying.

Conversely, when you do the same things over and over and in the same environments, it's easy to zone out. Your brain isn't being required to assimilate new information into its existing model. You're not being challenged by necessity to figure things out. Hence Napoleon Hill has said, "A good shock often helps the brain that has been atrophied by habit."

When you expose yourself to new ideas, new experiences, or things you've long feared, you will have what social scientists call a *disorienting dilemma*. This often occurs when people travel to foreign countries, but it can even happen by doing activities you've never done before. A disorienting dilemma is when your current mental model is somewhat shattered through exposure to new ideas or experiences that contradict your current way of thinking.

Being disoriented and experiencing a transformational learning experience doesn't mean you lose faith in everything you once believed, though. Rather, it's about weeding out ineffective and unhealthy ways of thinking and seeing. For instance, when you travel to a foreign country, you may realize that you held prejudices against certain types of people that were frankly incorrect.

The more novelty you can embed into your life and environment, the more engaged you will be. The more connections you make in your mental model, the more you'll have to draw from in the work you do. The wider and more unique the connections, the more innovative your work can be.

Is your routine the same every day? If so, how can you change things up? When things are new and different, even if it's just moving your furniture around, it's much easier to be present to the moment, rather than mindless and apathetic to routine and sameness.

SUMMARY

You can create enriched environments through the use of forcing functions. The most powerful forcing functions are:

- high investment;
- social pressure;
- high consequence for poor performance;
- high difficulty; and
- novelty.

In what ways can you begin embedding these environmental components into your own life?

Chapter 10

MORE THAN GOOD INTENTIONS

How to Adapt to New and Difficult Environments

A young student once asked the philosopher Epictetus how he should act in every situation. Epictetus responded, "It would be better to say, 'Make my mind adaptable to any circumstances.'" In our world of quick fixes and hacks, people are becoming increasingly conditioned to need very specific instructions to do just about everything. In a continually changing world, people need to become more adaptive, yet most are becoming less so.

Being adaptive is all about how you learn. It's about being mindful of your environment and about how to mine your environment of its best information and resources. Moreover, being adaptive is about controlling your environment, rather than having it control you. If you're a truly adaptive learner, you won't get stuck in one environment for long. You'll quickly learn what your environment has to offer and then transcend to new and more difficult environments.

Just like in a video game, you don't advance to the next level until you beat the level you're currently on. In a game, you may have to start over several times until you learn the lessons, overcome the obstacles, and beat the level. So, too, in life, lessons are repeated until they are learned. If you haven't successfully adapted to your current environment, you'll have a hard time adapting to more challenging ones. Consequently, this chapter will break down exactly how you can adapt to any environment, no matter how difficult.

The core concepts involved in being an adaptive learner include the following:

1. Having faith that you can adapt and change, or what psychologist Carol Dweck calls the "growth mind-set." This runs contrary to having a "fixed mind-set" and involves being a flexible learner, which means you don't get stuck in repetitious learning habits and using a select few learning styles.
2. Committing 100 percent to the change you seek, which means you're willing to *change who you are* to uphold or achieve your commitment.
3. Learning how to develop tolerances to the things you fear most.
4. Learning how to deal with and even embrace difficult and unpleasant emotions. This involves what psychologists call *emotional regulation* and requires you to directly expose yourself to your fears and resistances.

BECOMING A FLEXIBLE LEARNER

If you want to achieve something, you must first conceive and believe you can have that thing. Put more directly, you need to have faith in something that is currently intangible to you. This isn't a religious type of faith, but a conviction and belief that you can achieve your goals. If, for example, you want to become a millionaire, you'll need to believe you can become a millionaire and then *learn how to operate like one*. People who don't believe they can do something have a fixed mind-set. These people have been oversold on the idea of having a domineering "identity" that cannot change. Nature is god and nothing can be nurtured.

Unfortunately, years and years of research continues to show that people with a fixed mind-set struggle in life. They have lower self-esteem. Why wouldn't they? They believe they are stuck and can't do anything about it. Their fate was set at birth. Moreover, the research shows that people with a fixed mind-set have a really, really hard time *learning*. Why learn if you don't believe you can actually evolve? Those who have a fixed mind-set avoid difficult environments. They have one way they are comfortable learning and avoid situations that require different approaches and *learning styles*. Being adaptive to difficult environments requires that you learn and leverage multiple learning styles.

According to fifty years of research on learning theory, we all have a dominant *learning style*. We all also have several backup learning styles we rely on when we're in a difficult situation. However, there are also several other learning styles that each of us neglect and avoid. Some of these learning styles include the following:

- **Imagining**: coming up with ideas
- **Reflecting**: learning about the ideas you come up with
- **Analyzing**: synthesizing what you've learned and making strategic plans about what to do with those ideas
- **Deciding**: making a decision on ONE WAY you will go with a specific idea
- **Acting**: DOING SOMETHING toward the attainment of your idea
- **Experiencing**: learning from multiple angles, whether that be with other people or by creating something, failing, or attempting

If you skip any of these learning styles, you're not likely to get very far. But that's exactly what we all do. We all have learning preferences. We all prefer to do things "our way."

Interestingly, most people have a "growth" mind-set about the learning style they are comfortable with. For example, if you like math and learn in analytical ways, you probably believe you can get better at math. You approach challenges and failures as opportunities to grow. You seek out mentoring, education, and help. You're curious and seek to expand your knowledge and horizons about math. However, most people have a fixed mind-set about the learning styles they aren't comfortable with. If you don't like writing, you probably believe you can't get better at it. There are some things YOU simply can't learn. They aren't in your DNA or something, right?

If you have a growth mind-set, you operate with faith. You believe in something you can't see. You believe you can actually get better at something, even though that growth is currently visible only in your mind. If you have a fixed mind-set, you aren't operating with faith. You don't believe in what you can't see. You're a doubter. You're overconfident and overcommitted to a certain "cognitive commitment," or way of seeing yourself. Because you don't believe you can learn something, you actually can't. You've put yourself in a box and you have no vision for the future in that area.

However, psychologists and learning theorists have plenty of evidence now showing that you can *learn* any of the learning styles. But only if you're a flexible and adaptive learner. This changes everything. It changes the notion of each person having fixed "strengths" and "weaknesses," and instead paints a far more compelling picture.

You don't have strengths or weaknesses per se; instead you have positive or negative *learning habits*. These habits have been fostered throughout your life. They've been conditioned over and over by your environment, because it is your tendency to put yourself into situations you are comfortable with. To compound your unhealthy and overdeveloped approach, you do everything you can to create situations and environments that allow you to exercise that learning style. You avoid situations and environments that would have you do differently. All of these things are fluid, not fixed. Thus, all of these patterns can be shifted. Once shifted, you will be changed biologically and psychologically.

Conversely, if you believe you can learn anything, you can.

Are some things going to be harder to learn than others? Of course. Not because of fixed strengths and weaknesses. But because of atrophied or underdeveloped learning muscles, sabotaging beliefs, and bad habits. You learn new things by putting yourself in difficult and new situations that force you to become a flexible learner. This is the essence and foundation of being adaptive.

Learning new things requires making mistakes, looking and feeling dumb, and having to rework our worldview to see things from a higher vantage point. Hence, learning new things is very difficult and is the reason people avoid doing it. If you're serious about becoming an adaptive learner, you need to master the rare skill of commitment.

When you commit to learning, you commit to changing. This requires faith and a growth mind-set. Committing 100 percent is required because the process of deep learning is emotionally and intellectually difficult. Only those who are fully committed will endure the purging process of learning. Thus, the rest of this chapter will equip you with the knowledge and skills you'll need to become an adaptive learner. These skills include making a commitment, developing tolerances, adapting to your fears, and properly dealing with unpleasant and challenging emotions.

COMMITTING 100 PERCENT TO THE CHANGES YOU SEEK

Surfing big waves is a very different sport from surfing small waves. When surfing big waves, the consequences for failure are much higher. Actually, there's a chance you could even die if you're not successful. As IndoSurfLife.com reports:

"It takes a certain type of person to want to surf big waves, when the horizon goes black and a huge wall of water is bearing down on you, you have to want that wave in order to make it! If you hesitate or aren't fully committed you are going to get eaten!"

In order to catch and ride a big wave, you must be 100 percent committed. If there is any hesitancy whatsoever, you will fail. You may even fail if you fully commit. But the only way you might succeed is if you're dead set on seeing it to the end.

There's a useful lesson from big wave surfing that applies to a number of contexts in our lives. When you're fully committed to something, you have a different posture than if you're only partially committed. When partially committed, you're hesitant. You're not confident. You're unsure and undetermined. However, once you become dead set on something, all of the mental fog goes away. You become clear on what you're doing and why you're doing it. You stop thinking about the other options available to you. As Dr. Barry Schwartz has said in the book *The Paradox of Choice*, "Knowing that you've made a choice that you will not reverse allows you to pour your energy into improving the relationship that you have rather than constantly second-guessing it."

An amazing example of making a choice that could not be reversed happened in AD 711, when the Muslim forces invaded the Iberian Peninsula. Once his force landed on the foreign land, the commander, Tariq ibn Ziyad, ordered his ships to be burned. While his ships were up in flames, Tariq gave the following speech to his men:

> My Dear brothers, we are here to spread the message of Allah. Now, the enemy is in front of you and the sea behind. You fight for His cause. Either you will be victorious or martyred. *There is no third choice. All means of escape have been destroyed.*

This has become an apocryphal story. But whether or not it actually happened is beside the point. The point is this: The boats are burned. All means of return or escape or quitting have been eliminated. Can you imagine what it might have felt like to be a soldier in that army at that moment? You'd know that the choice was simple: win or die. How many of us avoid creating those kinds of stakes for ourselves?

You need to be 100 percent committed if you want to successfully and quickly adapt to a new and challenging environment. The question is, how do you become 100 percent committed? That's the very question I've been studying throughout my doctoral research as an organizational psychologist. Specifically, I've studied a concept I call "the Point of No Return," which is the moment it becomes easier to move toward your goals than to avoid them. Actually, your point of no return is the instant that pursuing your highest ambitions *becomes your only option*. You're fully committed to what you want to do, and this commitment creates a deep sense of confidence and congruence.

How does this work?

One of the most widely accepted theories explaining the relationship between biology and psychology is the bio-psychological theory of personality proposed by Dr. Jeffrey Alan Gray in 1970. Gray proposed two systems governing all behaviors:

Behavioral inhibition system: Your behavioral inhibition system is what attunes you to risks or threats in your environment. When you perceive these risks or threats, your behavioral inhibition system *stops you from acting.*

Behavioral activation system: Your behavioral activation system, on the other hand, is what attunes you to rewards. When you perceive these rewards, your behavioral activation system *encourages you to action* so you can obtain the reward.

These two systems are in constant tension with each other. In every situation, one of these systems is overruling the other. Either you are acting or you are inhibiting action. Either you are proactively *approaching* something, or you are trying to *prevent* something from happening. Offense or defense.

Most people have an avoidance orientation toward life. They aren't acting according to their deepest desires. Instead, they're playing it safe. They're calculating their moves to ensure they don't look stupid. They're hedging their bets, creating several backup plans in case their dreams don't quite work out. Ironically, they end up dedicating the majority to their backup plans, and that becomes their life.

Can you shift orientations if you've built your life around avoiding negative repercussions or emotions?

Of course you can.

You can change your very identity, because your identity

follows your behavior and the environments in which you place yourself. If that's the case, then what is the most potent behavior you could perform to shift yourself from playing life on defense to playing life on offense?

Primarily, a point of no return experience is initiated in the form of a financial investment, which forces the person to move forward out of compulsion. The financial investment is the capstone of a person investing lots of time and exploration in an idea. The moment significant amounts of money are spent on the idea, the investor can no longer return to their prior life. Their identity gets wrapped up in the investment. It becomes a part of them. It's how you go from being a wannabe at something to actually seeing yourself as that thing.

In psychology and economics, this behavior is explained by a concept called "escalation of commitment." According to the literature, escalation of commitment is an irrational decision that people make, primarily because they want to justify their initial decision or investment. Thus, sunk cost is at the heart of overcommitting to something. As stated previously, you can leverage sunk cost bias for your benefit in the form of precognition. Knowing that high investment will produce enormous inner commitment, you can produce your own point of no return.

And that's exactly what the highest achievers in the world do.

They aren't dreamers.

They're doers.

Because they have skin in the game.

When someone invests in themselves or their dream, their

commitment becomes solidified. Once invested, the person's identity and complete orientation toward their objective changes. Because they now *must* go forward, they're no longer confused about what they need to do. They're no longer uncertain if they're going to act in desired or undesired ways. They've *already* acted, and now they need to make good on that action. And there are several psychological reasons why they need to make good on that action:

- To not lose their investment
- To be consistent with the behaviors they've performed (hint: Identity follows behavior, not necessarily the other way)
- Because they truly want to achieve a particular goal, and they've now created external conditions that will eventuate in a self-fulfilling prophecy

Here's my favorite narrative from my master's thesis, in which I interviewed several entrepreneurs and wannabe entrepreneurs.

The main difference?

Entrepreneurs had experienced some form of "Point of No Return" experience, whereas wannabe entrepreneurs hadn't created such experiences. One of the people I interviewed was a seventeen-year-old kid who wanted to sell shoes. He and his "partner"—one of his high school friends—invested $10,000 in a shipment of shoes. Here's how he describes his "Point of No Return":

Yeah, once we had all of our money in the same inventory it was all or nothing. That really scared me, just knowing that it was like do or die. I had to sell the shoes. You couldn't turn back; you couldn't just get rid of them and get cash back; you had to go forward.

My follow-up question was, "Did anything change after this moment?"

Here's what he said:

After that, once I realized that we were truly going and everything, I think it really just opened me up to what I was able to do. At that point, I was like okay, I actually started a company, I've invested in it, and now I need to run this thing. That's when I think I really saw that I was running the company. It really changed my leadership role, I think, with my partners.

Once you've passed your point of no return, you've fully bought into your own vision. You're committed. Your role, and thus identity, changes. You've removed alternatives that were nothing more than distractions anyway. You've forced your own hand and now must move in the direction you want to go. You're all in. The act of investment changes you. It changes your proximity to certain people. It changes your posture toward your dreams. It changes how committed and convicted you are about making your decision come to fruition.

Brilliant things happen for you after you've crossed the

threshold of decision and commitment. Things seemed to fall into place in almost a mystical manner. As William Hutchison Murray has said:

> That the moment one definitely commits oneself, then Providence moves too. All sorts of things occur to help one that would never otherwise have occurred. A whole stream of events issues from the decision, raising in one's favour all manner of unforeseen incidents and meetings and material assistance, which no man could have dreamt would have come his way.

BECOMING VERY COMFORTABLE IN NEW AND UNCERTAIN SITUATIONS

Humans are extremely adaptive. We become desensitized and develop tolerances quickly. Psychological research has found that many people have developed a tolerance for vulgarity, violence, and sex on television due to constant exposure. Many people have developed tolerances for stimulants and other drugs. Because we live in a consumer society, our tolerance levels can get *way out of whack*. We eat sugar-loaded foods that distort our taste buds so that eventually we stop enjoying wholesome and healthy foods. We accept joint pain, headaches, and bloating as our homeostasis. We spend twelve to sixteen hours per day sitting in a chair staring at a screen. We've grown accustomed to astronomical levels of artificial dopamine flowing through our systems.

People can develop a tolerance and adapt to anything, even their fears. Purposefully developing a tolerance for one's fears is what psychologists call *systematic desensitization*. You can systematically desensitize to anything by exposing yourself over and over until you develop a tolerance. Eventually, you reframe your mental model and adapt, becoming a new person. Things that used to paralyze you with fear can become a normal part of your day-to-day experience.

For most people, the idea of waking up every day at 4:30 a.m. and immediately going to the gym seems crazy. Yes, the first few weeks or months might suck. But when it comes to adaptation, you don't really need to "work your way up." Rather, you can put yourself through the ringer and adapt to something extreme. For example, if you're wanting to make a habit of waking up at 4:30 every morning, you don't have to start by waking up at 6:00 for a few weeks, then 5:30 for a few weeks, then 5:00 for a few weeks, then eventually make your way to 4:30. You can jump in, feel the pain, and adapt.

This approach to adaptation is like slowly getting into a swimming pool one step at a time. You're delaying and compounding the pain because you're overly focusing on and extending it. What you focus on expands. Stop obsessing about the pain and instead focus on the result of what you're trying to do. When you jump right into the pool, you compress the shock and transition into a small amount of time. Although this approach is emotionally extreme, very quickly and instinctively your body acclimates to its new environment. Within twenty seconds, you've adjusted and the pool is no longer cold. Why did you spend so long ag-onizing over getting in? It wasn't so bad, right? You're now adapted. Psychological research has found that the anticipa-tion of an event is almost always a more charged emotional experience than the event itself. Almost always, you imag-ine it will be far worse than it ever really is. Then you extend that pain by procrastinating action. If you would just act, the pain would be far less severe and over before you know it.

Adapting to a new behavior like waking up early obviously takes longer than twenty seconds. But the same principle ap-plies. If you commit 100 percent and jump fully in, you'll adapt very quickly. However, you will experience an immedi-ate high level of emotional shock. You're not trying to soften the blow like when you ease your way into the pool. In-stead, you're willing to fully experience the purging process of weeding out old patterns and behaviors. And that purging process can hurt as you adapt to something better.

This principle of compressing the adapting process applies to all walks of life. In the phenomenal book *The Life-Changing Magic of Tidying Up*, Marie Kondo explains that the only way to truly overcome the addiction to consumption is by remov-ing all of the clutter from your environment in one fell swoop. You need to reset the environment, rather than continually trying to manage a broken system.

What have you been avoiding taking action on?

What swimming pools are you tiptoeing your way into?

Are you compounding the pain by overly focusing on your fears?

When are you going to fully jump in?

The moment you jump in with full commitment, you *will* realize it was much easier than you formulated in your mind. You will begin to adapt. But in order to do so, you'll need faith that you can do this, and you'll need to be a flexible learner. Even still, it will not be smooth sailing. Although exposing yourself directly is the fastest and most practical way to learn, it involves far more risk than the traditional and theoretical approaches. You'll have to actually deal with your fears and emotions. Which brings us to the next skill you'll need to master to become an adaptive person.

DEALING WITH AND EVEN EMBRACING DIFFICULT AND UNPLEASANT EMOTIONS

A branch of psychology known as *positive psychology* was born around the year 1998. At that time, there were only 300 research papers on the subject of happiness. Before that point, most psychologists were primarily interested in psychological illness. In 2017, there are now over 8,500 research papers on the subject of happiness. Happiness, it seems, is hot. Which is ironic, of course, because this is the precise moment in human history when happiness often seems more elusive than ever.

Focusing on the positive side of psychology has been very beneficial for society. However, there are many psychologists who are extremely frustrated by the scope and focus of the research being done in positive psychology. These scholars believe the majority of research in positive psychology has been overly simplistic and has ignored crucial elements of the human condition. According to Dr. Paul Wong, a renowned positive psychologist, the core premise of positive psychology has been that *good emotions lead to good outcomes and negative emotions lead to negative outcomes*. The result of this premise is that people have come to believe they must always feel good, or something is wrong. This might relate to the spike in prescription drug use over the past two decades. Rather than dealing with problems, people are avoiding them and numbing themselves.

Positive psychology is rooted in a *hedonistic worldview*, which advocates the avoidance of pain and pursuit of pleasure. Unfortunately for those who have fully bought into positive psychology and its findings, a life of pleasure-seeking is not what creates a deep sense of meaning and satisfaction. It's the load, the challenge, and the opposition that create true fulfillment and accomplishment. True happiness often involves taking a hit in the present to pave the way for the future.

Momentary pleasure and true happiness are two very different experiences. As scientist and spiritual leader James Talmage wrote, "Happiness leaves no bad after-taste, it is followed by no depressing reaction; it brings no regret, entails no remorse. True happiness is lived over and over again in memory, always with a renewal of the original good; a moment of pleasure may leave a barbed sting, [as] an ever-present source of anguish."

Ancient philosophies such as stoicism and spiritual beliefs

such as Buddhism and Christianity fundamentally oppose a hedonistic approach to life. Embracing challenges, pain, and difficulty are among the primary paths to meaning and growth according to these perspectives. Rather than a hedonistic worldview, ancient philosophy and most spiritual perspectives embrace a *eudemonic worldview*, which advocates seeking a virtuous and meaningful life of growth and contribution.

Currently, there is a movement occurring known as the *second wave of positive psychology*. The researchers involved in this new movement emphasize this eudaimonic view. They embrace both the positive *and negative* sides of life, seeing both as essential to optimal outcomes for individuals and societies. They offer the following things as valuable pieces of living a full and complete life:

- Delayed gratification
- Discomfort
- Frustration
- Dissatisfaction
- Pain
- Tragedy
- Awkwardness
- Embarrassment
- Uncertainty

These feelings aren't necessarily enjoyable in the moment. However, these and other unpleasant emotional experiences often produce incredible outcomes. It is only by going through difficult and challenging experiences that you can evolve. If you constantly avoid pain and mask your emotions, you'll never grow.

Best-selling author Jack Canfield once said, "Everything you want is on the other side of fear." And he's right. But I'm going to take it one step further. Pain, discomfort, shock, boredom, impostor syndrome, awkwardness, fear, being wrong, failing, ignorance, looking stupid: Your avoidance of these feelings is stopping you from a life greater than your wildest imagination. These are the feelings that accompany a life of success. And yet, these are the very feelings most often avoided. They are avoided because, as stated previously, most people have developed an extreme avoidance orientation toward life.

Even still, wealth, optimal health, incredible relationships, and deep spiritual maturity are all available to everyone. But there is a price to pay to have these things. The primary obstacle in your way is *how you feel about what you need to do*. Most people aren't willing to feel difficult emotions on a regular basis. However, if you're willing to disregard how you feel in the moment, you'll have access to a world of opportunity unavailable to 99 percent of the population, who are only concerned about *now*.

When you're fully committed to something, the negative emotions and experiences along the way are expected. They are even welcomed, because you know rough emotions are the very speed bumps that will stop most people. You also know that those are the very experiences that are purging your old weaknesses. You're releasing your suppressed emotions and evolving into a new and better person. And very quickly, the experiences that were once emotionally trauma-tizing become routine and sometimes even pleasant.

CONCLUSION

Being an adaptive learner is all about mastering your envi-ronment. The only way for you to master new and difficult environments is to force yourself out of your shell and habits. Yes, you have a learning preference, or way of doing things. But "your way" will keep you stuck. Instead, you should mindfully assess the situation at hand and do *what is required*.

If you have plans of making rapid strides in your personal evolution and success, you'll need to create scenarios with enormous challenge and responsibility. In order for you to rise up to the situations you put yourself in, you'll need to be 100 percent committed, just as if you're riding a big wave. The fastest path to this level of commitment is investing in yourself and your decision. You'll also need to embrace un-certain situations, which will require you to actually seek and approach difficult emotions.

Chapter II

GROW INTO YOUR GOALS

Outsource Your Motivation to
High-Pressure Environments

> If you're a true competitor, you always feel that
> pressure to attack and conquer. You thrive on it.
> You intentionally create situations to jack-up the
> pressure even higher, challenging you to prove
> what you're capable of.
>
> —Tim Grover

John Burke is a twenty-nine-year-old pianist from At-
lanta, Georgia. In 2017, he was nominated for a
Grammy for the Best New Age Album. One of the
songs on that album is entitled "Earth Breaker" or as Burke
calls it, "Finger Breaker." It's an intensely fast and ferocious

song. Burke's goal for "Earth Breaker" was to create the experience of being in an earthquake.

Here's the interesting thing: It was a song that Burke didn't even know he could write when he started it. In fact, that idea is one of Burke's core approaches to songwriting. When he composed the music for "Earth Breaker," he couldn't actually play the piece. Physically, it was too fast and beyond his current skill level. But that's exactly what he wanted. He wrote a song he couldn't play and then practiced over and over and over until he could do it. Writing a song beyond his skill level acted as a forcing function for Burke. It created conditions with more advanced rules than he was accustomed to living. He had to grow into the environment he created for himself.

Like many other world-class performers, Burke thrives on pressure. He purposefully embeds several layers of external pressure into his environment, which continually forces him to show up day after day and create. It isn't just picking songs that are a level or two above his skill. He goes much, much further. The moment he decides he's going to pursue a new project, such as writing a new album, he immediately decides when it will be completed and released. Once the release date is determined, he works backward, mapping out all the key milestones along the way. He calls his piano studio engineer that very day and gets on his schedule, usually three to four months in advance, for the day he will record the album. He pays up front to ensure he gets his spot, but also uses that investment as a forcing function to actually create the album and be in a position to record it on the scheduled date.

Then he organizes his personal calendar and schedules in "creation time" throughout his workweek over the next several months. He considers these scheduled times for writing music as important meetings. Consequently, if something pops up during those creation times, like a gig or collaborative opportunity, he says his calendar is already booked for that time. He willingly passes up great opportunities because he has creation time on his schedule. It's an almost unbelievable level of commitment for a field—songwriting and music production—in which a lot of people sit around wait for the muse to visit them.

And it isn't just internal mechanisms, either. Burke commits publicly as well, borrowing from strategies we've already discussed. Now that his schedule is complete Burke jumps on his social media accounts and begins telling his fans about his upcoming album. This "creates an expectation," Burke told me. He highly values the trust of his fans. So, by creating the expectation up front, he adds another layer of commitment. He doesn't want to let his fans down. He then tells his close family and friends in person about his goal.

Here's the truly shocking thing: All of this happens the *same day* he decides he's going to start a project. This is why he's been able to so prolifically compose seven albums by the age of twenty-nine. Burke creates conditions that force him to succeed. He operates by a set of rules that facilitate high creativity and achievement. Thus, his success is calculated and his outcomes are predictable, because they are the consequence of the factors he strategically engineers into his situation. Beyond productivity, Burke's use of forcing functions allows him to continually produce better and better music. He is always attempting something beyond what he's ever done before. In order to do so, he embraces ambiguity, novelty, and high difficulty. When writing a new album, he immerses himself in genres of music he's unacquainted with. He pushes himself to learn new styles and techniques. He doesn't want his album to be easy to create. He wants the creation of each album to break him down—to humble him—so he can rise higher than he's ever risen before.

How can you create conditions that increase the pressure in your life?

COMPETE ABOVE YOUR SKILL LEVEL

> It is the most closely-allied forms, varieties of the same species, and species of the same genus or of related genera, which, from having nearly the same structure, constitution, and habits, generally come into the severest competition with each other.
>
> —Charles Darwin

According to Charles Darwin, all forms of life compete with those most similar. It would make little sense for a painter to compete with a rock-climber. Rather, a rock-climber advances her skills by competing with other rock-climbers, generally of a similar skill level. In business terms, you compete with those in the same industry. And within that industry, the little players generally compete with the other little players, while the big players compete with the other big players.

Competing with those at your same level yields slow and minimal progress. You're better off "competing" with people far advanced to your current level. By so doing, you can quickly learn to live according to more advanced rules. In his book *The Art of Learning: An Inner Journey to Optimal Performance*, Josh Waitzkin shares how he applied this principle to become world-class at tai chi. When given unsupervised practice time, Waitzkin observed that most others in his tai chi class would naturally practice with those at their same skill level or slightly worse. This was done in many ways out of ego, because who wants to lose?

Who proactively makes their life difficult? Not very many people. But Waitzkin did. He lives by a rule he calls "investing in failure." While at practice, he would purposefully train with people far more skilled than he was. In so doing, he would get the crap kicked out of him, over and over. However, this process compressed and quickened his skill development. He could experience firsthand the abilities of those often years ahead of him. The mirror neurons in his brain allowed him to quickly mimic, match, and counter his superior competitors. Thus, he progressed much faster than others in his class.

According to the new science of genetics known as *epigenetics*, the signals from your environment are responsible for your genetic makeup far more than the DNA you were born with. Dr. Steven Cole, the director of the UCLA Social

Genomics Core Laboratory, has said, "A cell is a machine for turning experience into biology." Your current genetic makeup is the product of your environment and thus is always changing. Obviously there are limits (at least at this point) to the extent you can change your biology. You can't make yourself seven feet tall. But psychologically, you can become a completely different person. And your psychology and biology are inseparable.

Rather than "competing," with people at your perceived skill level, compete with those who are where you want to be. In other words, always punch above your weight. Herein lies a fundamental difference between those who become successful and those who don't. Unsuccessful people make decisions based on current circumstances while successful people make decisions based on where they desire to be.

Competition is actually a powerful form of collaboration. When your competitors perform in their peak state, you are required to deliver your best work and stretch to even higher standards. You are propelled forward by their creativity and ingenuity. Competing with the highly skilled can be an exhilarating experience as you discover skills you had never manifested before. In tennis, for example, when one player is on fire and sending insane balls over the net, that forces the other player to *respond*. Thus, when your competition is playing out of their minds, it brings something new and better out of you.

Your talent doesn't exist in a bubble. What you can accomplish is the product of the situation in which you find yourself. Hence, who you decide to compete with is incredibly important.

It's more energy-consuming competing with the huge herd of average. But spending energy and performing at your highest level are not the same thing. Actually, they are often in direct conflict. While most people are content competing with amateurs, you want to compete with only the best in the world. No matter which field you're in, just pretend like what you're doing is playing tennis. Those at the top of your industry are across the net from you, sending you fireballs. How are you going to respond?

If you can get your head in *that game*, and actually believe you can "compete" at that level, you'll see the "experts" work from a different angle. You'll stop worshipping your heroes and their work. Instead, you'll begin *studying* them. What exactly are these people doing differently? How was their work crafted and marketed? Where are the holes you could easily improve upon? What aren't they doing and why? Rather than consuming your hero's work as a spectator, you should see it as a tennis ball being sent over the net toward you. Your job now is to respond by sending something back even better.

COMPETE IN PUBLIC

Competition is a powerful way to bring out the best in people. A prime example is the "space race" between the Soviet Union and the United States that started in 1955. For those years, it meant something amazing to be an American. Going to the moon mattered greatly to everyone. The very challenge and competition created a scenario that facilitated rapid innovations and progress, not just in aerospace engineering, but in many other fields as well. Actually, Americans probably haven't seen progress so extreme since then, as the public competition isn't as fierce. In a famous speech given in 1961, President John F. Kennedy said (emphasis mine):

Recognizing the head start obtained by the Soviets with their large rocket engines, which gives them many months of lead-time, and recognizing the likelihood that they will exploit this lead for some time to come in still more impressive successes, *we nevertheless are required* to make new efforts on our own. For while we cannot guarantee that we shall one day be first, we can guarantee that any failure to make this effort will make us last. We take an additional risk by making it *in full view of the world*, but as shown by the feat of astronaut Shepard, this very risk enhances our stature when we are successful.

Competition was powerful. But racing to the moon in front of the whole world was even more powerful. In a similar way, author and leadership coach Darren Hardy tells the story of taking a cycling class outdoors near a beach in San Diego. This particular cycling class had each bike electronically connected to a huge projector screen. Each person had a personal avatar connected to their bike that was then displayed on the projector, showing their name and a picture of their face.

Once the cycling class started, the projector showed in order who had gone the farthest/hardest on the bike in bold red letters. There were around fifty people taking the class and only the top fifteen or twenty people's names and faces showed up on the projector. Not only could the other people in the class see the giant projector, but so, too, could random people who walked by or were chilling on the beach. Hardy said he's never worked so hard in a cycling class. The rules of this particular situation made high performance inevitable.

CONTEXT-BASED LEARNING: WHY MENTORSHIP IS MORE EFFECTIVE THAN FORMAL EDUCATION

The military and several missionary programs use a learning and teaching method known as "context-based learning" to radically accelerate the learning process. Context-based learning occurs in a social situation where knowledge is acquired and processed through collaboration and practical use, not merely the dissemination of information from a teacher. In order for this knowledge to be acquired, a learner engages in a real-life task, not a theoretical task. The skills the learner develops clearly match and naturally translate into real-world settings.

Learning through doing is far more powerful than sitting in an abstracted and sterile environment and reading textbooks, as is the practice in formal education. Aside from being highly practical, relevant, and experiential, context-based learning is powerful because it generally involves individual coaching and immediate feedback on performance. When you mess up on the task, you can get coached on how to do it better. You can then continue to practice repetitiously until your skills become automatic and sub-conscious.

Here's a breakdown of how context-based learning works:

1. You learn a concept at surface level.
2. You practice and use that concept in a real-world scenario to solidify and contextualize your understanding.
3. You get immediate coaching and feedback to smooth out your rough edges.
4. You repeat over and over with greater intensity and shorter timelines to produce automaticity.
5. You get more coaching and feedback to assess your knowledge and skills.

Interestingly, researchers examined the effects of role-playing on the self-concept of shy adolescents. One group of adolescents got traditional discussion-based training while another did role-play-based training. The group that did role-plays experienced a significant positive change in their self-concept, which had a significant impact on their behaviors. In our digital world, simulation training—based on role-playing real-world scenarios—is becoming increasing popular. Additionally, research has found that getting consistent feedback is essential to effective learning.

HOW TO APPLY CONTEXT-BASED LEARNING

True learning is a permanent change in cognition and/or behavior. In other words, learning involves a permanent change in how you see and act in the world. The accumulation of information isn't learning. Lots of people have heads full of information they don't know what to do with.

If you want to learn something quickly, you need to immerse yourself in that thing and immediately implement what you're learning. The fastest way to learn Spanish, for instance, is by immersing yourself in a Spanish culture. Flash cards for fifteen minutes a day will eventually get you there. But you'll make deeper connections with a few days fully immersed than you would in months of "dabbling."

You need enough clarity to have high motivation to move forward. The more clarity you have of the path set before you, the more motivated you'll be to go down that path. Thus, rather than trying to motivate yourself, your goal should be to clarify the next few steps ahead of you.

HIRE A MENTOR WHO IS BRILLIANT AT WHAT YOU WANT TO DO

If you don't pay for something, you rarely pay attention. Most people want stuff that's free. But if you haven't invested your money, resources, or time, it is incredibly difficult to invest yourself.

How much do you invest in yourself?

How much of yourself have you invested?

How committed are you to yourself?

If you aren't investing in yourself, then you don't have any skin in the game of your own life. If you aren't invested in your business, you probably won't do high-quality work. If you're not invested in your relationships, you're probably more focused on what you can get than what you can give.

When it comes to self-improvement, investing 10 percent of your income on yourself will yield a hundred-times-or-more return on that investment. For every dollar you spend on your education, skills, and relationships, you'll get at least a hundred dollars back in returns. If you want to do something extremely well, you need to surround yourself with the right mentors. High-level goals require high-quality mentoring. If you suck at something, it's because you haven't received quality mentoring in that thing.

The best mentorships are the ones in which you pay your mentor. Often, the more you pay, the better, because you'll take the relationship far more seriously. You won't purely be a consumer. Instead, you'll be invested, and as such, you'll listen more carefully. You'll care more. You'll be more thoughtful and engaged. There will be higher consequences for not succeeding.

I invested $3,000 to get help writing my first book proposal from a highly successful writer. That $3,000 got me maybe four or five hours of his time. But in those four or five hours, he taught me what I needed to know to create an amazing book proposal. He provided me resources that dramatically enhanced and sped up my process. With his help, I was able to get a literary agent and eventually a major book contract. Had I been overly concerned about the $3,000, I'm confident that to this day, I'd still not have written a book proposal. At the very most, I'd have written a terrible one. I would not have been as motivated or invested, so I would have been far more likely to procrastinate in taking needed action.

If you don't have much money, surely you can afford to buy a book. How much money and time do you spend on entertainment, clothes, or food? It's a matter of priority. It's only when you invest in something that you have the motivation to make it happen. Beyond mentorships, you should invest in education programs such as online courses, events, and books. Your level of success can generally be directly measured by your level of investment. If you're not getting the results you want, it's because you haven't invested enough to get those results.

The greatest benefit you'll get by hiring a mentor is that you'll be left with a feeling of *dissatisfaction* with your work. Even if you've produced something far beyond anything you've ever done before, your mentor will be quick to point out just how far you still need to go. Thus, even when you complete a project, or advance in skill, you'll be left with a feeling of *wanting more*. This is the exact feeling you need to have, because it will lead you to double down on your craft, going deeper and deeper into the mechanics and principles of what you do. Your upgraded thinking and vision will inspire in you an urgency to improve your skills.

Experiencing dissatisfaction toward your life and current work is a reflection of personal evolution. This can be a painful and humbling process. Yet your dissatisfaction is not a lack of gratitude, but a heightening of expectations and personal standards. You're no longer okay with your current situation and outcomes. You now expect and want more for yourself. Your vision has expanded through experience and training. As Oliver Wendell Holmes, Jr., said, "A mind that is stretched by a new experience can never go back to its old dimensions." You want more. And although in the moment you may feel discouraged, you know your dissatisfaction with what you have is a sign you're on the up-and-up.

REPETITION UNTIL YOUR LEARNING BECOMES UNCONSCIOUS (OUTSOURCED TO ENVIRONMENT)

While I implemented what I learned, my teacher would watch me from a distance. He let me struggle as I tried to remember what he had just shown me. The first time, applying what he taught took a lot of time and effort. So we did it again, and again, and again. Over time, I became competent and thus confident.

Learning something new is all about memory and how you use it. At first, your prefrontal cortex—which stores your working (or short-term) memory—is really busy figuring out how the task is done. But once you're proficient, the prefrontal cortex gets a break. In fact, it's freed up by as much as 90 percent. Once this happens, you can perform that skill automatically, leaving your conscious mind to focus on other things. This level of performance is called *automaticity*, and reaching it depends on what psychologists call *overlearning* or *overtraining*. The process of getting a skill to automaticity involves four steps, or stages:

1. Repeated learning of a small set of information. If you're playing basketball, for instance, that might mean shooting the same shot over and over. The key here is to go beyond the initial point of mastery.
2. Make your training progressively more difficult. You want to make the task harder and harder until it's too hard. Then you bring the difficulty back down slightly, in order to stay near the upper limit of your current ability.
3. Add time constraints. For example, some math teachers ask students to work on difficult problems with increasingly shortened timelines. Adding the component of time challenges you in two ways. First, it forces you to work quickly, and second, it saps a portion of your working memory by forcing it to remain conscious of the ticking clock.
4. Practice with increasing memory load—that is, trying to do a mental task with other things on your mind. Put simply, it's purposefully adding distractions to your training regimen.

Essentially, you want your understanding of something to be fluid and flexible. You want to be able to apply your learning in different contexts and for different purposes. Thus, you learn your skill inside and out.

EMBED SEVERAL LAYERS OF TRACKING (OUTSOURCE ACCOUNTABILITY TO ENVIRONMENT)

> When performance is measured, performance improves. When performance is measured and reported, the rate of improvement accelerates.
> —Thomas S. Monson

Accountability really is where the rubber meets the road. It rarely exists in most environments. Few people are kept accountable for their behaviors in their working and personal relationships. Few people even keep themselves accountable.

In order to combat people's aversion to accountability, I created a yearlong online course with a new module every week. Within each module, I provided homework assignments, such as writing down personal goals or removing specific distractions. I challenged the members to track their morning and evening routines. One week, I surprised my audience by making that week's module exclusive. Only those who could provide clear evidence that they'd been tracking their morning and evening routine were given that week's content.

Many of the people taking my course were pumped up and excited by the increased intensity. They thanked me for having the integrity to hold them accountable. Several people emailed me and said it was a turning point for them. It challenged them to actually print out the homework assignment from the week before and mark off their calendars. By creating consequences for their behavior, they were forced to do the work they paid to do in the first place. By going through the motions of the actual process, they saw the value of tracking their progress and reporting in their journal (and then to me) how they were doing on a daily basis relative to their goals.

Of course, not everyone liked the wrench I threw into their online course. One person emailed me in frustration. "Are you saying I can't have the content I've already paid for? I must be misunderstanding you," he fumed.

"No, you're not misunderstanding me," I said. "I told you when you purchased this course that it was set up different from other courses. Rather than giving you all the information up front, I've made this an experiential learning process. What you're dealing with right now, these emotions and frustrations, *that* is the content of this course. It's not just videos and PDF printouts. It's meant to challenge your actual behavior. So, no, you can't have the content unless you are accountable."

Once I made this shift in the course, it immediately separated those who were committed to growth from those who were information consumers. By creating a learning environment with rewards and punishments, several people got back into the course who had fallen off months prior. Their internal flame was reignited by a higher set of external expectations. Despite a few people being disgruntled by the changes, most people emailed and thanked me for "taking the course to the next level."

We all want to improve our lives, especially when we've invested in personal development.

Now that you are invested in more than half of this book, how different is your physical environment?

How have you changed your learning environment?

How are you making yourself accountable?

What are you outsourcing to your environment?

What forcing functions have you put in place?

Have you increased the pressure to succeed?

JOIN A MASTERMIND GROUP (OUTSOURCE SUCCESS TO ENVIRONMENT)

> We are kept from our goal not by obstacles but
> by a clear path to a lesser goal.
>
> —Robert Brault

If you want to achieve big things, your path will be unclear and hazy. The emotional need for clarity and fear of the unknown leads people to abandon their dreams for more straightforward pursuits in less demanding environments. Having goal clarity is essential to high motivation. Consequently, in order to increase your motivation, you'll need to embrace uncertainty until you've gotten enough clarity to move forward.

However, "clarity" does not mean you have it all figured out. It means you're clear *on the next step or two*. If you're at mile marker 1 and your dream is at mile marker 50, you just need enough info and support to get to mile marker 3 or 4. Once you get there, you'll need further instructions. But you have no clue what those instructions will be, because you don't currently know what you don't know. When you get to the next step, you'll be able to ask better questions. You'll better assess who can help you get to mile marker 5, 6, 7, or 8.

You're on a treasure hunt and you're finding clues and guides along the way. Uncertainty and difficult emotions lurk behind every corner. This is the process and emotional experience of pursuing a big dream. You'll be stretching, growing, and moving while most other people are overwhelmed by the distance between mile marker 1 and 50. While they're staring at the forest from a distance, you're winding your way through the trees. And soon enough, you'll be on the other side.

This entire approach to learning and growth is *experiential*, not theoretical. Rather than having all the answers, you want just enough information to move forward. The fastest way to get relevant information is through failure and real-world experience. Your environment for success can't be a classroom or a therapy couch. It has to be in the trenches of experience. Environmental design for powerful learning involves experience in real-world situations. These situations are inherently challenging, the stakes are high, and the consequences immediate. Additionally, your training is practical, not theoretical, and you're getting feedback and coaching from mentors and experts. This is the most challenging and painful way to learn, and thus it is also the most effective.

In 2014, my aunt Jane joined Joe Polish's exclusive and

high-level Genius Network mastermind group. The purpose of Genius Network is to provide an environment where "industry transformers" can connect, collaborate, teach, and help each other.

After going to a few of the Genius Network events, I could see a tangible difference in Jane. She had more confidence, clarity, and focus. She was far more bold and smart in the marketing she did with her company. One of the core philosophies of Genius Network is ten-times thinking. When you think ten times bigger, you're forced to rework your faulty assumptions and directly face your fears head-on. For example, if you are currently making $50,000 per year and set a goal to make $500,000 the following year, you're going to have to radically change your entire approach to life and business. This is a healthy transformation that can't occur with incremental growth methods.

Joe Polish very seriously implements the idea of ten-times thinking. When a new member joins Genius Network, they invest $25,000 in their yearly membership. Members are then expected to increase their income by $250,000 within that year or they cannot sign up for Genius Network the following year. If you don't get ten times your initial investment, then Genius Network isn't a good fit for you.

In 2014 when Jane joined, I was just starting my PhD program at Clemson University. To say I was jealous would be an understatement. I determined during that time that I would eventually become a Genius Network member myself. Many of my role models were a part of that group. I wanted to be their peer, not just an admirer. But at the time, I had never even written a blog post. I certainly hadn't made any real money. But I had a dream.

Jane gave me a Genius Network tag that I strapped to my backpack. Every day while walking on Clemson campus, I was thinking about Genius Network. That tag was an external reminder, a trigger, of my goal of one day joining the mastermind group. But I didn't want to join solely for the sake of being around my role models. I wanted to contribute to the network.

In July 2017, after having grown a significant online platform and learned some very useful marketing skills, I decided it was a good time to apply for the group. The $25,000 investment was somewhat intense. After all, I was still a graduate student, and we were paying my tuition out-of-pocket. But in all honesty, I knew that the group would provide me with the motivation, connections, and skills to fulfill the ten-times requirement. I also knew that my ten-fold return wouldn't be purely financial. In fact, immediately upon becoming a Genius Network member, I felt like I had a new identity. The goal I had thought about and worked toward for three years had now become my reality. I had done what I needed to do to "get in the door" and become a part of a highly selective environment.

Simply being in an environment isn't enough to be completely transformed by it, though. So I made clear strategic plans before joining the group about how I could maximize the experience. As with all transformational experiences and relationships, the focus cannot be on yourself. Instead, you need to have an abundant mentality, where you generously and genuinely do all you can to help others. As Joe Polish frequently states, "Life gives to the givers and takes from the takers."

Consequently, once registered and paid, I immediately signed up to speak at the next small-group meeting in Arizona. I hired and worked extensively with Joel Weldon, a public speaking coach, to ensure I delivered my best strategies in the most effective way. I wanted my talk to be so easy and actionable that people would be naturally motivated to implement the principles. I used my journal as a visualization tool, in addition to several sessions with Joel.

The environment I worked to create during the talk was manifested better than I had hoped. Following that meeting, I was invited to share the same ideas at the annual event just two months later. Again, I contemplated how I could now offer the most value to the four hundred people who would be in attendance.

Ultimately, knowing the importance of this book, *Willpower Doesn't Work*, I desired to provide advance copies of it to as many of the influencers at the November 2017 Genius Network annual event as possible. That was only three months away and the editors still didn't have a solid draft for the March release. When I presented my plan to my editor at Hachette, she was initially quite surprised. "We usually only print twenty or so for our authors," she told me. I was requesting four hundred.

I knew what I wanted and had a white-hot *why*. My goal was to get this book and the ideas as expansively distributed as possible. When your why is clear and powerful enough, your strategy will inherently be bold and clever. Being completely dead-set on my vision, I created conditions that made the achievement of my goal certain. I continually considered what more I needed to invest in the achieving of my goal and made sure everyone knew my level of commitment to the goal.

My passion must have shined through to my editor. After sharing my plan to distribute the four hundred advance copies (and why this conference was such a crucial date to hit), my editor received approval for the early copies. If necessary, I would have paid for them myself and driven up to New York in my car to get them. Nothing was going to stop me. The multiple investments I had made in my book reshaped my psychology. Through the process of upgrading my environments through these investments, I became the author I wanted to become.

No matter which environment you're in, there will be what psychologists call a "normal distribution," which means most people will be relatively the same. There will be some outliers on both ends of the spectrum, those who aren't performing as well as the norm and those who are radically outperforming the norm.

Being an adaptive learner is all about never getting stuck at a certain level in your development. You want to leap into a demanding situation and allow that situation to reshape your identity. You do this by taking on a new role and absorbing the culture of your new environment. You take everything you're learning and immediately apply it. By applying what you learn, you'll quickly elevate yourself to the norms of your new environment.

For instance, if you make a large investment to get mentoring or training of any sort, the investment itself only serves as the motivational mechanism to compel forward progress. The investment is a forcing function, hopefully a point of no return. This point of no return is not a destination, but a point of departure. It's the moment at which you become fully committed to the changes you want to make. Thus, you need to ride the motivation of your investment to apply everything your new environment provides you. You need to transform yourself to become what your commitment entails.

As you immediately apply, you'll change. You'll improve, and then you'll want to expand your horizons. You'll begin to see where the "cap" of your new environment is, and then you'll discover how to transcend that cap. You don't want to get stuck in a single environment for too long, just as you don't want to get stuck with a single mentor too long. To quote Lao Tzu, "When the student is ready the teacher will appear. When the student is truly ready, the teacher will disappear."

Being an adaptive learner means you're never getting stuck at a single stage. Every stage has rules and lessons. And lessons are repeated until learned. Far too often, people plateau at a certain stage in their development, and then over-adapt to a specific environment. They become accustomed to a set of rules and become content with the outcomes or consequences of living those particular rules. Herein lies a reason most "successful" people have a very hard time becoming more successful. As author Greg McKeown has pointed out, success becomes a catalyst for failure.

Don't drink it in.

Don't become content with the results you've gotten and the progress you've made. Acknowledge how far you've come. But don't get stuck there. Instead, continually surround yourself with more advanced teachers and competition. Continually upgrade your standards for the quality of work and contribution you can make. Never develop a fixed mind-set. You are fluid. There's no end to how much you can change.

Have you plateaued?

Are you complacent and comfortable in your current environment?

Are you satisfied with the benefits of what surrounds you?

ANOTHER REASON WILLPOWER IS A FALLACY

Attending a Genius Network event is like drinking out of a fire hose. You literally cannot consume or synthesize everything you're being taught. It's like ten hours straight of very high-level marketing and personal development training, two days back-to-back. It's exhausting. Yet, at the same time, it's rest and recovery from daily routines and work. And here's where the willpower research is yet again defective.

According to research, your willpower is basically your energy stores. Once you run out, you're out. Yet research on mindfulness done by Ellen Langer has found that the very act of changing environments can dramatically increase your energy. So, by leaving your regular environment and engaging in even more demanding work, like being at a Genius Network event, you should have plenty of energy, because you're in a new and novel environment. And novelty, after all, is one of the primary forcing functions that evokes a high state of flow.

SUMMARY

The goal of this chapter was to make motivation and willpower irrelevant. When you create enriched environments of positive stress and high demand, your motivation to succeed is sky-high without any conscious effort on your part. You are not in conflict with your environment but being pulled forward by it. The specific strategies detailed in this chapter for outsourcing your motivation to enriched environments included:

- Installing several layers of external pressure and accountability;
- Making your goals public;
- Setting high expectations for customers and fans;
- Investing up front on your projects and scheduling them in advance;
- Surrounding yourself with people who have higher personal standards than you have;
- Competing with people who have a much higher skill level than you do by viewing competition as a form of collaboration;
- Making a commitment and then practicing or performing

these in public settings. The external pressure of performing for others only heightens your internal pressure
to succeed;

- Getting enough clarity to move forward a few steps toward your goal;

- Hiring a mentor who is world-class at what you want to
do; and

- Joining a mastermind group filled with role models and
people who will help you elevate your life.

Chapter 12

ROTATE YOUR ENVIRONMENTS

Change It Up Based on the Work You're Doing

The environment you're in should clearly match the behavior you're doing. It is for this reason that you shouldn't have a TV in your bedroom. Your bedroom isn't for watching TV. Even if you live in a small apartment, you're better off having a TV in the kitchen or even the bathroom. Although there's a disconnect in having a TV in a kitchen or bathroom, it's not as detrimental as the sleep you're losing because your bedroom is designed to require willpower.

A primary reason people have a difficult time sleeping at night is because they are environmentally triggered to do a lot of other things when they enter their bedroom. However, for optimal sleep, your bedroom should be filled with triggers specific to getting good sleep. There should be no distractions to that goal. It's helpful even to have clothes designated specific for sleep that you wear nowhere else. This, too, can serve as a trigger, prompting you to get sleepy.

Just as your bedroom should clearly reflect the behaviors you're going to do in that environment, the physical spaces in which you work should also match the work you're going to perform that day. Increasing numbers of people are working on computers, yet doing a wide variety of tasks on those computers. Doing all of those different tasks in the same physical space is not the optimal approach. Instead, there should be different environments in which you work, which clearly link to the type of work you're doing. Each environment should trigger the mental state needed to do each type of work.

THE MYTH OF THE EIGHT-HOUR WORKDAY

The traditional nine-to-five workday is poorly structured for high productivity. Perhaps when most work was physical labor it made sense to work such long hours, but it doesn't make sense in the knowledge-based working world we now live in. Don't believe me? Just look at the effects of this poorly structured working *culture*. It is common—even expected—that employees have mediocre performance, addiction to stimulants, lack of engagement, and even hatred for their jobs. These are not causes, but effects of a bogus environment for work in the twenty-first century.

Many organizations and entire countries have realized the

change in workflow as most work has shifted from manual to mental work. As a result, many organizations have shortened work shifts to thirty hours per week and now allow employees to work remotely, knowing that a cubicle is often not the best environment for mental and creative work.

The traditional nine-to-five is a clear example of society operating by a set of rules that no longer make sense in the new system. The world has changed. If we want to be successful, we need to understand the new rules of the system and optimize our lives to successfully execute those rules. The new rules of today are that ideas and creativity are the most sought-after and profitable skills.

The best creative work requires a blend of intensely tight focus for one to four hours, followed by a relaxed mind wandering in a *different* environment from where you were doing intensely focused work. You need to rotate your environments. In one study, only 16 percent of respondents reported getting creative insight while at work. Ideas generally came while the person was at home, in transportation, or during recreational activity. "The most creative ideas aren't going to come while sitting in front of your monitor," says Scott Birnbaum, former president of Samsung Semiconductor.

When you're working directly on a task, your mind is tightly focused on the problem at hand (i.e., direct reflection). Conversely, when you're not working, your mind loosely wanders (i.e., indirect reflection). While driving or doing some other form of recreation, the external stimuli in your environment (like the buildings or other landscapes around you) subconsciously prompt memories and other thoughts.

Because your mind is wandering both contextually (on different subjects) and temporally between past, present, and future, your brain will make distant and distinct connections related to the problem you're trying to solve (eureka!). Creativity, after all, is making connections between different parts of the brain. Ideation and inspiration are processes you can perfect.

When it comes to creative and mental work, rather than working according to arbitrary social norms, such as nine to five, it's best to work according to your highest and best energy levels. According to psychologist Ron Friedman, the first three hours of your day are your most precious for maximized productivity. As he stated in a *Harvard Business Review* article: "Typically, we have a window of about three hours where we're really, really focused. We're able to have some strong contributions in terms of planning, in terms of thinking, in terms of speaking well."

Research confirms the brain, specifically the prefrontal cortex, is most active and readily creative immediately following sleep. Your subconscious mind has been loosely wandering while you slept, making contextual and temporal connections. A solid practice for capturing the subconscious breakthroughs you experienced while sleeping is to immediately begin journaling when you wake up. During this journal session, it's best to dump your thoughts onto the paper as they relate to what you're trying to accomplish, such as specific goals.

However, it's important to not be too tightly focused during this journal session, as you want to allow your mind to somewhat wander wherever it goes. This wandering may lead to the very breakthroughs you had while sleeping. I have been using the method of morning journaling for nearly ten years. While writing in my journal, often outside the gym while in my car, I get ideas about articles I'm going to write or people I need to reach out to. Many of my relationships began with an idea from a journaling session, which then led to actively reaching out and, over time, cultivating a transformational relationship.

In order to maximize this experience even further, you can become proficient at directing your subconscious mind-wandering while you sleep. Inventor Thomas Edison said, "Never go to sleep without a request to your subconscious." While transitioning from being awake to being asleep, your brain waves move from the active beta state into alpha and then theta before eventually dropping into delta as we sleep. It is during the theta window that your mind is most receptive to reshaping your subconscious patterns. Just before falling asleep, think and visualize about what you want your mind to focus on as you sleep.

ROTATING ENVIRONMENTS FOR INCREASED ENERGY, PRODUCTIVITY, AND CREATIVITY

Although research has shown that you aren't likely to get more than three to five hours of high-quality mental work each day, you can do things to either extend that window of opportunity or ensure you get those precious hours of flow.

According to several studies by Harvard psychologist Ellen Langer, a simple practice of rotating "the context" can keep your mind far more active.

In one of her experiments, she had a group of people perform a writing task using the same colored pieces of paper, usually white. In the other group, the people performed the same task, but the pieces of paper alternated colors, such as going from white to yellow to white to yellow. This small and simple environmental tweak kept people more active and engaged.

Doing the same thing for extended hours in the same environment can become mentally stale. You need novelty to keep the brain active. You need a timeline to keep you on your toes. You need difficulty to keep yourself open, humble, and effortful. If you notice yourself zoning out or purposefully distracting yourself, you need to step into a new environment. Often, the very act of walking into a different room will facilitate a flood of ideas related to the work you were just doing. Even better is if you take a short mental break and then continue your work in a different environment, whether that means going to a different room, changing your chair, or going somewhere entirely different for a few hours.

NEVER WORK IN THE SAME PLACE TWO DAYS IN A ROW

Author and entrepreneur Ari Meisel is keenly aware of how his environment affects his thinking, emotions, and ability to perform his work. He's extremely detail oriented, and even fine-tunes things like the lighting in every environment he's in to trigger the mental state needed to accomplish what he's trying to do. Meisel has broken up his workweek to never be in the same environment two days in a row.

As an entrepreneur, he does many different types of work, from writing blog posts and recording podcasts to creating physical products and doing consulting calls. He has a designated day of the week and work space to optimize the specific type of work he's going to do that day. Also, in order to get far more done, he buckets activities together that are related. On blog-writing days, he writes ten blog posts and nothing else. On podcast-recording days, he and his partner sometimes record five or more episodes.

The following is a breakdown of Meisel's workweek:

Mondays and Fridays

On Mondays and Fridays, Meisel works at the Soho House in New York City. He claims the Wi-Fi is bad there, as is the cell phone service. This is to Meisel's favor, because on Mondays and Fridays, he's completely zoned into writing and other forms of content creation. Additionally, the lighting at the Soho House is darker and deeper, creating a kind of cave-type feeling. This increases Meisel's focus, as he's less likely to be distracted by bright lights and other people.

On these highly creative workdays, Meisel eats almost nothing until he's completely done. There's lots of research to back this up: Focused work is often easier on an empty stomach. To quote productivity expert and entrepreneur Robin Sharma, "Eat less food and you'll get more done." Of course, this isn't true of all types of work, but highly relevant for deeply cognitive and creative work. A full stomach can fog up your mind.

Finally, Meisel has highly specific Pandora stations for the work he does on Mondays and Fridays, which he only uses at Soho House while doing his creative work. This music acts as another trigger to sink him deeper into his flow state. He generally listens to electro swing music, specifically the "Caravan Palace" Pandora station. He generally loops the same twenty songs over and over while listening on noise-canceling headphones.

Listening to classical, ambient, or electronic style music while doing creative work is a norm for many artists and entrepreneurs. Additionally, unlike Meisel, who loops the same twenty songs, many people (myself included) often listen to the same song on repeat for several hours while working. In her book *On Repeat: How Music Plays the Mind*, psychologist Elizabeth Hellmuth Margulis explains why listening to music on repeat improves focus. When you're listening to a song on repeat, you tend to dissolve into the song, which blocks out mind wandering (let your mind wander while you're away from work!). WordPress founder Matt Mullenweg listens to one single song on repeat to get into flow. So does author Tim Ferriss and many others. There are websites such as listenonrepeat.com that allow you to loop YouTube videos.

Tuesdays

For Meisel, Tuesdays are designated for making calls and holding meetings. He spends a lot of time both on the phone and doing video chats. This work is far more energetic and social than the work he does at Soho House. As a result, he works at his partner, Nick's, apartment. The moment Meisel walks into Nick's apartment, his brain clicks into social mode. He and Nick have a highly synergistic relationship, which gets the ideas going while they are talking to clients and doing meetings. They want to be in physical proximity to each other so that before and after meetings, they can discuss. Moreover, while each of them are on the phone with a client, the fact that there's a physical audience keeps them working at their highest level.

On days he works at Nick's apartment, Meisel doesn't wear his blue-blocker sunglasses. He doesn't bring his headphones. And he strategically eats lots of healthy fats in addition to proteins, fruits, and vegetables to keep his energy going. Doing social and energetic work is best done with food in the body.

Wednesdays

On Wednesdays, Meisel works in a coworking space in New York City that he pays $99 a month to be a part of. On this day, he does lots of video and phone calls similar to the work he does at Nick's apartment the day before.

Thursdays

On Thursdays, Meisel doesn't have a designated space assigned. Thursday is more fluid, depending on what projects he has going at the time. Sometimes he'll have meetings, which will influence where he works. Often, he'll go to a recording studio and spend five hours recording seven to eight podcast episodes.

HOME ENVIRONMENT

Meisel doesn't work at all while at home. Like having a TV in the bedroom, working at home can create a mismatch in environmental triggers, which can block you from living in the moment. Meisel wants to be completely engaged and *at home* when he's home. As a creative person, he naturally gets lots of ideas wherever he is. Consequently, one of the main aspects of his home environment is having several devices and means for capturing ideas.

The longer you let an idea sit in your mind without putting it on paper or in some other form, the more it taxes your short-term memory. Meisel has an Amazon Dash Wand for recording thoughts when they pop in his head. Those thoughts may be related to work, or they may be as simple as "We need to order something from Amazon." He also uses his Alexa a lot for recording ideas. Voice recorders are strewn throughout his house because often he's doing a task where he can't use his hands. That way, even while he's changing his child's diaper, he can capture an idea the moment it enters his mind. He takes this capturing a step further than a lot of people: In his shower, he uses AquaNotes, a waterproof notepad to capture all the ideas that appear while he's showering.

For Meisel, his entire process can be broken down into three key strategies: optimization, automation, and outsourcing. His first goal is make things function well and to remove anything in his environment or life that lags. Once everything is optimized, he automates everything he can with the use of technology. Unlike most people, who have become the slaves and addicts of tech, Meisel is an incredible example of someone who uses tech to expand his reach and to increase his time *away from work* so he can actively engage with his family. After everything in his life has been automated, he outsources whatever is left. The only thing Meisel doesn't automate and outsource is his superpower—that skill and ability that only he can do. The rest he has someone else or a technology do for him.

CONCLUSION

Your environment is part of your work. Every environment has rules, and clearly some environments are more optimal for certain types of activities. You should work in environments that trigger you into the mental state needed to do the various types of work you do.

Additionally, to increase your level of engagement, you

should continually be switching your working environments. You don't need to go to completely different locations throughout your workweek like Meisel does. Simply changing rooms every few hours or for varying tasks will do wonders.

Also, provide yourself needed mental breaks between intensely focused work sessions. These mental breaks should not be spent surfing the Internet in distraction mode. Instead, you should leave your workspace and walk around. If you can go outside or expose yourself to lots of external stimuli, such as trees and people, all the better. While relaxing, your mind will wander and begin to make distant and distinct connections related to the work you're doing.

If you rotate and alternate your working environments, you will have a great deal more energy. You won't get bored or distracted as easily. You'll get far more creative insights. This works really well when you batch activities with specific environments. Do a whole lot of *one* activity on a single day and in a single environment. This is very different from how most people work. Most people work in the same environment and are constantly switching from task to task. Thus, they aren't optimizing their environment and they're never getting into flow.

Chapter 13

FIND UNIQUE COLLABORATIONS

Design Your World Through
Who You Work With

Some rules can be bent, others can be broken.

—Morpheus

In the science-fiction novel *Ender's Game*, the main character, Ender, is a young boy who is recruited by the government and taken to an orbiting space school where he's trained to become a military leader. The core training modality is in the form of a highly competitive "game." Like Ender, there are several other children being trained at the space school. These kids are all on teams where they compete in a highly sophisticated battle room. In the lunchroom where all the kids eat, there is a giant electronic scoreboard listing the teams from best to worst in descending order. The competition is fierce.

Ender, it turns out, is head-and-shoulders more adaptive than all the other kids, even those several years older than he. He has a high tolerance for ambiguity and thus is not disoriented in new situations. He's very aware of his changing environments, and unlike the others, he realizes that orientation in zero gravity is purely relative. There is no set up and down. However, Ender notes that the other armies persist in maintaining the orientation of gravity environments after entering Zero G.

Because the rules in Zero G are different from the rules in the corridor leading into the battle room, Ender's quick adaptation becomes a huge advantage. According to Dr. Ellen Langer, Harvard psychology professor and the head of the Langer Mindfulness Institute, mindfulness is nothing more than awareness of context, as well as awareness of variability or alterations in that context. If you're mindless, then you don't notice nuance. You assume everything is black and white. You assume the rules in one environment are the same as the rules in another. You also incorrectly assume you are the same person from one environment to the next and thus are less likely to see your own role and have the ability to alter that role.

Ender used his understanding to radically manipulate the game to his advantage. He destroyed the other teams by targeting their mindlessness in Zero G. Having never seen anything like this before, the other teams didn't know how to respond. However, it didn't take long for them to learn what

Ender was doing. And in due time, the culture of the battle school and of the game was forced to change.

Most people operate under very limiting and incorrect assumptions. Very few people mindfully see what others don't. Like the fleas in the jar, most people operate under the dogma of groupthink. The social culture, as inaccurate as it is, prevails. And people are blinded by cultural norms. Just as important, people incorrectly assume these norms are unalterable. Every environment is an ecology, and thus, every environment is fluid, malleable, and alive.

UNIQUE CONNECTIONS SHATTER NORMS

> The day before something is truly a breakthrough, it's a crazy idea.
>
> —Peter H. Diamandis

In 1905, Albert Einstein published four research articles, known as the Annus mirabilis papers, that went on to substantially alter the foundation of modern physics regarding space, time, and matter. Interestingly, when Einstein published these papers, he was not working in an academic setting, but rather at the Swiss patent office. His work in this counterintuitive environment allowed him different reflective angles and questions than a typical physics lab. The connections Einstein was able to make led to innovative and scientific breakthroughs that altered how humanity now sees the entire world and cosmos.

Take another highly influential entity (arguably THE most musically influential and culturally innovative band of the twentieth century): The Beatles. The Beatles' primary talent was their ability to make unique connections. Music theory professor David Thurmaier explains, "Above all, the Beatles remained curious about all types of music, and they continually reinvented their own music by injecting it with fresh influences from multiple cultures. This experimentation adds a dimension to their work that separates it from their contemporaries' music."

Beyond incorporating and mashing ideas from a vast array of sources, the Beatles were also systematic at collaboration. John Lennon would sketch out ideas, or fragments of a song, then pass the ideas to Paul McCartney to improve or finish. Paul would do the same. One of the pair might add a middle eight or bridge section to the other's verse and chorus. Lennon described their synergy as "writing eyeball-to-eyeball" and "playing into each other's noses." Often, two incomplete songs emerged into a masterpiece through this process.

Thus, far from how most people imagine creativity—as uncontrolled and somewhat unpredictable, occurring in isolation—the Beatles had a functioning system. Paul McCartney recounts: "As usual, for these co-written things, John often had just the first verse, which was always enough: it was the direction, it was the signpost, and it was the inspiration for the whole song. I hate the word but it was the template." Collaboration is the physical act of making new and novel connections. When two or more people work together toward a shared goal, the output of their work is different from the sum of the inputs; the whole varies from the sum of the parts. Connections are made by two distinct sources that would likely not be made from fusing other sources.

The Beatles' ability to innovate was not random. They were highly talented, well-trained, and well-versed musicians. By integrating unique influences into their environment, they were able to creatively push beyond the boundaries set by others. As Pablo Picasso once said, "learn the rules like a pro, so you can break them like an artist."

As will often be the case, people will initially be repelled by your forward thinking. They won't understand the connections you're trying to make. However, if you can persuasively bring a number of ideas together and distill them into a simple concept, eventually the new idea will catch hold.

Once new ideas take hold and become pervasive throughout an environment, that environment changes. In a cyclical way, the new environment then reshapes the people. As Winston Churchill said, "we shape our buildings; thereafter they shape us." When the Beatles changed the environment, the new environment then went on to change culture and humanity.

THE POWER OF UNIQUE COLLABORATIONS

You never change things by fighting the existing reality. To change something, build a new model that makes the existing model obsolete.
— R. Buckminster Fuller

There's a key concept some of the best entrepreneurs are leveraging extremely well. "Unique collaborations" (sometimes referred to as *co-branding*) can create a scenario in which the knockout strengths of each business, idea, or person, when combined, result in "one plus one equals ten."

In 2017 my wife and I went to Peru to eat at the famed Central, a restaurant that is often ranked in the top five best in the world. The reservations were exclusive and the dining experience unique. But what fascinated me most was the collaboration between Chef Virgilio and his botanist sister Malena. Virgilio shared with me that once he had his idea for bringing all the elevations of Peru into his kitchen, he knew he needed his sister's collaboration. She wasn't working in the food industry and was not an easy sell. He crafted the perfect culinary trip to New York to convince her. He knew that with her on his team they would create something nobody had ever done before.

Additionally, one of Virgilio's core concepts is to find ambitious people in unexpected locations. When he gets his car fixed, he looks at the mechanic and asks, "Is this mechanic ambitious?" When he spots ambition, he knows that by moving it to his environment, he can transform people into amazing chefs and waiters.

Another example, the GoPro combination with Red Bull resulted in "Red Bull Stratos," a space diving program. Thanks to GoPro and Red Bull, on October 14, 2012, Felix Baumgartner flew approximately twenty-four miles into the stratosphere over New Mexico in a helium balloon before free-falling in a pressure suit and parachuting to Earth. The total jump, from leaving the capsule to landing, lasted approximately ten minutes. Baumgartner free-fell for four minutes and nineteen seconds before pulling his rip cord.

This event would not have happened without the collaborative ideation of GoPro and Red Bull. Their strengths were evenly matched. They both brought amazing contributions to the table in the form of technology, philosophy, audience, and objective. The whole became new and different than anything either of them could have concocted on their own. As a result, world records were shattered, new technology was developed, and millions of people around the world were both entertained and inspired.

Steve Down, a serial entrepreneur, is brilliant at creating unique collaborations that reshape industries. In 2015, Down started a restaurant chain called Even Stevens. He borrowed an idea from the shoe company TOMS, which provides a pair of shoes to a person in need for every pair bought. At Even Stevens, for every sandwich bought, a local hungry person gets a free sandwich.

When Down initially had the idea, he began asking friends and others in the restaurant industry what they thought. However, he was quickly disappointed by the responses. The restaurant industry has tight margins and budgets. Very few restaurants are profitable, let alone new restaurants. So how could a new concept possibly succeed while simultaneously providing hundreds of thousands of free sandwiches per month to hungry people?

Had Down spent a large period of time in the restaurant industry, he probably wouldn't have attempted to start something like Even Stevens. It went against every convention and rule in the industry. But Down came from a much different background, and thus had very different notions and strategies about creating and scaling businesses. With a background in finance, he spent a lot of time running the numbers. He met with several local nonprofits and eventually came to a profitable conclusion about how he could create a socially conscious restaurant that makes a positive impact on the community.

In the past three years, over fifteen Even Stevens restaurants have popped up in Utah, Idaho, and Arizona. Nearly every one of these restaurants became profitable within thirty days of being open. Each Even Stevens is teamed up with several nonprofits in close proximity. The proceeds from each sandwich are administered to a nonprofit that then buys in bulk the sandwich supplies needed to feed the local hungry. It's a profitable and clean system. It's also a very unique collaboration between a for-profit organization and local nonprofits.

According to Down, the only way the Even Stevens concept would work is if the food was outstanding. If the food wasn't good, people would think the whole thing was a gimmick. As a result, Down did a lot of up-front research on how to develop a world-class and "kraft" menu for a fast-casual dining experience. He hired a highly specialized and recognized chef to help him. Down wanted a unique and admirable concept to bring people in the door, but he wanted the food to blow people's minds. For the first three years Even Stevens was open, it successively won the title of Best

Restaurant and Best Sandwich throughout the entire state of Utah.

DEVELOPING YOUR OWN UNIQUE COLLABORATIONS

> Alone we can do so little; together we can do so much.
>
> —Helen Keller

If you play by the same rules as everyone else, your results will be average. If you read the same books as everyone else, you won't be able to develop unique conceptual arrangements. In other words, you won't be able to create new connections that end up reshaping the rules of your environment.

You can't get much work done if you have the lone ranger mentality. Independence shouldn't be the goal. Interdependence and synergy should be what you're after. The ideas you come up with on your own may be interesting, perhaps even brilliant. But the ideas you could come up with when collaborating with people from very diverse backgrounds and industries have the potential to completely alter the rules of what you're doing. When you develop unique collaborations, especially with people who have already succeeded big in their industry, you can go ten times or even a hundred times with your goals.

If you're not collaborating with people from diverse backgrounds who have radically different experiences, skill sets, and perspectives from you, then your chances of making bold and unique connections that change the world are very low. Most people compete with others at their similar skill level. Most people collaborate with others in their same niche who have a similar background. Their worldviews are too similar to those around them to break the rules of the existing norms.

INDEPENDENCE SHOULDN'T BE YOUR GOAL

According to former Harvard psychologist Robert Kegan, the majority of people advance from a "socializing" self to a "self-authoring" self. A socializing self is a state of complete dependence. When you're at this stage, everything you do is calculated to avoid fear and anxiety. You only do that which you believe others want you to do.

Self-authoring, conversely, is a state of independence. At this level of conscious evolution, your thinking becomes more complex. You've developed goals, plans, and an agenda. Everything you do, then, is to further that agenda. Relationships, for example, are a means to further your aims. If certain relationships are no longer serving your agenda, you remove them. This is the level of thinking that most self help encourages in people. Self-authoring individuals believe they are incredible. Better than others. They are on a quest to write their own narrative. And without question, that is a much better and more empowering proposition than living in a reactive and unconscious state.

Unfortunately, a huge drawback of self-authoring and

"independent" thinking is that you can't see past your own mental filter. And often your plans and goals aren't ideal. Yet, because you are hell-bent on achieving your particular goal, you reject or ignore information that contradicts or seems irrelevant to your schema. Even more, you believe your filter is the objective reality, or the way the world actually works.

Finally, Kegan explains the third and final stage of conscious evolution. Very few people reach this level of mental complexity. Going from dependent to independent is much easier than going beyond independence. Success is quite the impenetrable barrier to cross for most people. Kegan's third stage is the transforming self. At this, the highest step, you have a worldview, but you aren't "fused" to it. You can stand back from your mental filter and actually look at it from the outside. You can compare and contrast yours with other filters.

At the transforming-self stage, you both value a stance, analysis, or agenda and are wary of it. Accordingly, you are open to learning and feedback and are constantly seeking to adjust and improve your approach. What is right *is* far more important than *being* right. Context, then, determines what is right.

What was right yesterday may no longer be right today. You're adaptive but purposeful. Thus, like the authoring self, you have a map of where you want to go, but you're open to having that map modified, expanded, and possibly redirected entirely with better information. Rather than obsessing about a particular outcome, you expect the best outcome to occur.

Only when you transcend the authoring-self stage to

the transforming-self stage can you consciously experience the benefits of collaboration. Indeed, when you're at the authoring-self stage, you believe you are the sole cause of your success and thus remain ignorant of the fact that every thought you've had and goal you've pursued was shaped by your environment.

Once at the transforming-self stage, you purposefully avoid transactional relationships and seek transformational relationships. You don't know what new elements will be integrated into your system, but because your trajectory is upward, you're confident the changes will be better and different than you could ever imagine on your own.

From the vantage point of the transforming self, it seems both ignorant and negatively constraining to only see things *one way*. A single filter, no matter how refined, has its downsides. Especially in an ever-changing world. Furthermore, when you are stuck in a stage of independence, the depth and breadth of your personal evolution become stunted. You're not purposefully seeking to have your paradigm shattered by better thinking. You're not collaborating with people more experienced and with more expertise than you. You are so fixated on what you want that you can't see past it. Your ego stops you from being so much more than you could be.

Very few self-improvement products even hint at the transforming self as a possibility. Competition and independence *are* the primary goals for most individualistic thinking. The reason self-improvement products rarely teach at the higher and more contextual levels is simple: We live in a highly individualistic culture. The individual is the focus and the obsession. As a country, America is in peril of collapse because the greater whole and purpose have been forgotten. We are no longer a *united body* but a group of isolated individuals with no sense of the environment we've created. Unwittingly, that environment is now shaping us.

SUMMARY

Every environment and every industry operate under various rules. Those rules are not ironclad. Even physical laws, such as gravity, can be harnessed and manipulated. For centuries, the travel industry worked within the realm of gravity keeping people on the ground. The collaborations of scientists, innovators, and entrepreneurs have always shattered the "traditional" rules and replaced them with new and better ones. That's how both innovation and evolution work: reframing the rules, structures, and norms of an environment.

Across the globe, there is a huge push to be "independent." This comes largely from Western culture's obsession with individualism. As opposed to more Eastern cultural perspectives, Western culture views the self as singular and independent from context. This perspective, although empowering, is also naïve and false. Advances in technology have made the global interdependence even more apparent. We all rely on each other to do what we're doing, on personal, societal, and global levels.

Independence shouldn't be your goal, particularly if you're trying to change the world. The reason is simple: Your personal worldview is far too small and narrow. Your agenda, as inspiring and altruistic as it may be, is limited to your own agenda. If you combined your agenda with that of other people or organizations, your agenda would transform. It would expand and change in ways you can't presently comprehend, because the combination of ideas and people is the only way to actually form something original and new.

If you're willing to move beyond the pervasive ideology of independence and to fully embrace interdependence and transformational relationships, then you have the ability to not only crush your transactional-minded competition, but you also have a chance at shattering the rules and paradigms of the system in which you're operating. Reframing the rules, norms, and conversations in a particular industry is what all innovators want to do. Because, regardless of how well things are going, they can always be improved. And when you improve a system, you improve the lives of everyone in that system, even your competition. When you enhance the environment for your competition, you force them to think, create, and live at a higher level, which then forces you to up your game as well. Evolution at work.

Chapter 14

NEVER FORGET WHERE YOU CAME FROM

Remember the Environment Where You Began

Phiona Mutesi is a Ugandan chess player. She was born in 1996 in a suburb called Katwe, which is the largest slum in the city of Kampala. To say Phiona grew up poor would be an understatement. She grew up in a place where having a moped means you are considered wealthy. Most people in her slum have a handful of possessions to their name. Very few are educated. Most live their lives as laborers.

At the age of nine, Phiona dropped out of school because her mom couldn't afford to send her. She lived day to day selling corn on the streets. One day in 2005, she followed her brother around town in attempts to sell corn, and they stumbled upon a school run by Sports Outreach Institute, a

Christian and sports mission. The school offered free porridge and even free chess lessons. Phiona and her brother were hoping for some porridge, but immediately Phiona was seized upon by the game that dozens of young boys were playing in the school.

The school is a Christian mission project founded by Robert Katende, who fled Uganda's civil war as a child and was later orphaned. As an adult, he found a job with Sports Outreach, a nonprofit Virginia-based group that uses sports to spread Christianity. Every day from noon to 5:00 p.m., between a dozen and fifty children gather at the Institute to play chess, gossip, and listen to preaching.

Phiona and her brother started regularly going to the school to play chess. She fell in love and became obsessed with it. She couldn't read, and thus, Katende didn't expect her to learn some of the more complex chess positions. However, over time Phiona started displaying a high degree of understanding of the deeper components of the game. Soon she began beating the more affluent and trained players from different cities.

Eventually she was able to get out of her slums and experience more affluent sides of life. She was exposed to better food, nicer clothes, and more comfortable sleeping arrangements. These experiences changed her. Having started to succeed and develop a name for herself, she was no longer content with the menial work in the slums. Her mind had expanded and she wanted more for her life. Phiona's mother was upset at Katende for tainting her daughter, who no longer felt comfortable in her home environment.

For a long period of time, Phiona disconnected from home. She was caught in a limbo state, what best-selling author Jeff Goins has termed the "in-between." Like a lobster that outgrows its shell and must find a new one, you can feel naked and like a stranger. Phiona went on to become very successful, one of the best chess players in all of Uganda. Indeed, she evolved and was able to transcend her limiting environment and create a more expansive and powerful environment. She was able to learn new and better rules, which led her to getting educated, making a living, and being able to pull her whole family out of the slums.

Despite being changed throughout her experience, Phiona never forgot where she came from. She never forgot about the people she loved. She didn't put herself above them. Yet she didn't lower her standards in order to make her family feel comfortable. She lived her life to a much higher level and brought them up with her. She changed her own environment and then changed the environment of those she loved. She didn't let where she came from stop her from where she was going.

NEVER FORGET WHERE YOU CAME FROM

According to a fascinating 2013 *New York Times* article by Bruce Feiler, feeling connected to a family history can have a significant impact. In the article, Feiler references research done in the late 1990s by psychologists Dr. Marshall Duke and Dr. Robyn Fivush, who wanted to explore why families were falling apart more frequently—specifically, what "families could do to counteract the forces." Interestingly, around the same time, Dr. Duke's wife, Sara, who also happened to be a psychologist working with disabled kids, noticed something peculiar. "The ones who know a lot about their families tend to do better when they face challenges," she told her husband.

Why would this be?

This single insight led Dr. Duke and Dr. Fivush to explore familial remembering. They ultimately created a psychological measure called the Do You Know? scale that asks twenty questions. Example questions from the survey include:

Do you know where you grandparents grew up?

Do you know where your mom and dad went to high school?

Do you know where your parents met?

Do you know an illness or something really terrible that happened in your family?

Do you know the story of your birth?

After conducting research on many children and families, and comparing their results to a battery of psychological tests the children had taken, Dr. Duke and Dr. Fivush came to an overwhelming conclusion. The children who knew more about their family's history exhibited far greater control over their lives. They had far greater self-esteem and told a much healthier story to themselves about their family and history. The Do You Know? scale turned out to be the single strongest predictor of a child's emotional well-being and sense of happiness.

Interestingly, this research occurred shortly before the

September 11 terrorist attacks. Dr. Duke and Dr. Fivush decided to reassess the children from their research. The results were compellingly clear. To quote Dr. Duke, "Once again, the ones who knew more about their families proved to be more resilient, meaning they could moderate the effects of stress."

Interestingly, Dr. Duke has found that families generally have one of three unifying narratives they tell about themselves. The first is an ascending narrative, wherein a family talks about how far they've come from one generation to the next. For instance, "When our family moved to this country, we had nothing. Your grandpa didn't even go to high school. Now look where we are at." The second narrative is descending, wherein a family talks about where they once were, and how things have gone south. However, the third and most healthy narrative is oscillating, wherein a family talks about both their ups and downs.

According to Dr. Duke, knowing where you came from can give you "a sense of being a part of a larger family." Children have the most self-confidence when they have a strong "intergenerational self," which is knowing you are a part of something bigger than yourself.

According to management expert Jim Collins, human organizations of any form, whether families or companies, fare best when they are connected to their story of origin. Religions and other groups, such as the United States military, similarly leverage this key human need, the need to have context with something bigger than oneself, by continually emphasizing where the group originated. Traditions are established to *remember*.

Dr. Duke recommended that parents create similar activities with their children to embed a deep sense of personal history. Creating traditions, such as going on vacations, or doing certain things regularly as a family is very healthy for a child's development and long-term success in life. Even if a child grows up and doesn't continue the same traditions in their adulthood, they have a sense of family and history.

How can you apply this?

Don't forget where you came from. Not only that, learn more about your history and roots. You'll develop a far greater appreciation for the life you have. Again, you are not independent of your context. You are standing on the shoulders of giants. And the more you come to know someone, even if that someone is your diseased family members, the more empathy and love you will have for them. The more sense of history you have, the more sense of control you'll have over your life. The more context you'll have built around yourself. The healthier you will be.

Of course, learning about your history doesn't mean you must repeat that history. You can and should evolve beyond the previous generation. You're not fixed. You're not bound by "nature." You can change as you change your environment.

YOU'RE NOT BOUND BY YOUR PAST, BUT YOU SHOULD HONOR IT

One night, seeing the success of a recent article I wrote, I received this text from a relative: "You proceed with your works and words with such certainty, friend, and I applaud your confidence. Yet I would advise you, no matter how high your accolades, to remember WHAT you truly are." This text didn't surprise me at all. It is all too common to believe that people are fixed and unchangeable structures. What I was in high school, I will always be. What I was a birth, is how I will die. I replied to my relative that their belief and my belief about "what I truly am" are very different. I don't believe I'm fixed. I'm not constrained by the environment I was once trapped in. I chose something different and to become different. And I will never stop evolving and changing. Even still, it is extremely important to respect where I came from and to never forget.

The same is true for you.

No matter how "successful" or "evolved" you become (or think you've become), it is essential that you don't let it lead to egotism. You may learn how to operate according to very high-level rules that most people are completely ignorant of. Your regular environment may be an unfathomable dream to most people. The work you do may impact millions of lives. You may be happy and proud of all you've been able to do. However, if you take seriously the concepts in this book, you must realize that you are not the cause of your success. You are the product of your changing environment.

Every generation takes for granted the rules of the new system in which they live. For example, kids growing up today have zero comprehension of a world without smartphones and the Internet. They may mistakenly believe their ability to create and do brilliant things is solely the product of themselves. The more accurate truth is that they can do what they do because their environment allows them to. Their worldviews are shaped by the environment they live in. They stand on the shoulders of giants who have made enormous sacrifices to create the world around them.

In a similar way, you, too, stand on the shoulders of giants. You could not be where you are without the challenges you've faced, the mentors you've had, and all the many people who have created the world you live in. When you believe you are the sole cause of your success, you commit what psychologists call the *fundamental attribution error*. You attribute your success to yourself.

No.

Your success, in the way it happened, could not have happened without your environment. It was the situation and countless other people that made you. As entrepreneur Michael Fishman said, "Self-made is an illusion. There are many people who played divine roles in you having the life that you have today. Be sure to let them know how grateful you are. Example: the person who introduced you to the person who introduced you to your spouse or business partner or client. Go back that far."

Because you are not the sole cause of your success, you should be in a continual state of humility and gratitude. You didn't earn being born when you were. You didn't earn the Internet. You didn't earn your parents and mentors. You didn't earn all the sacrifices that have allowed you the *privileges* you have. And privileges you have in extreme abundance. These privileges are intended to be built upon. Use them! Leverage them! But never forget that they didn't come from you.

"Evolving" never means you're better than other people, especially those living according to rules that consistently produce negative outcomes. Just as you are fluid and not fixed, so is everyone else. You are never more valuable than other people. No one has an absolute value, but rather, we all have a relative value based on what surrounds us. People who may not be where are you could become what you are, if they had the surroundings that shaped you. Please don't commit the fundamental attribution error in believing that others could not do or be better than they are. Their situation has shaped them. They don't have a fixed and unchanging nature. They can be nurtured and reshaped. Even if they have dogmatic and inflexible views.

The best thing you can do is see people as you see yourself. You can change. You have infinite potential and flexibility, as do other people. Treat them that way. Love them, regardless of whether they violate your personal rules. Then dedicate the rest of your life to becoming the type of person who can reshape the rules of their environment, so they, too, can advance and elevate as you have done.

NO MATTER WHERE YOU ARE, YOU CAN CHANGE

'****ve spent the last decade relentlessly studying how human beings change. My search began originally from a spiritual perspective and continued during my undergraduate and doctoral studies as a psychologist. I'm continuing to study the most effective and permanent ways to make desired change.

This book was not meant to be a comprehensive tome. Instead, it was meant to quickly provide you a set of strategies for more effectively making the changes you want. If you've read this far, I know you want something bigger for yourself. You want to live more congruently with your highest aims and ambitions. You want to feel in control of your life, and you want to be transformed through powerful experiences.

From so many different perspectives, I'm completely confident that willpower is not an effective approach to personal change. Spiritually, I'd rather rely on my higher power than my own power. Motivationally, I'd rather rely on WHY power than willpower. And behaviorally, I'd rather outsource my willpower to a goal-enriching environment.

Does willpower work at the surface level? Of course. But only if you stop there. If you follow any attempts at willpower to their logical conclusions, it will lead to ruin. Eventually and always, a person will be forced to either adapt to their environment or entirely change it. If a person remains stubborn and strong-willed, they may continue their willpower approach throughout life. But it will be at the expense of everything else, and they'll be left internally conflicted, disease- and stress-ridden, and lonely. Their environment will have beaten them into submission. Sadly, this is the common path for most people. Rather than living in alignment with values through environmental design, most people attempt willpower and ultimately settle into a low-level, goal-conflicting environment.

I wrote this book primarily as an attempt to prove that you can change. You're not fixed. Rather, you are fluid. And you can actually change in some very radical ways. You can even change immediately. But you'll never be able to do that if you focus exclusively on yourself. The most honest and powerful way to change yourself is by leveraging your external environment. When you make an abrupt and intense change to your environment, you're forced to change yourself.

While growing up and during high school, I watched my

life begin to slip from my control. My parents divorced when I was eleven years old. Throughout junior high and high school, my life lacked stability. I felt like I had nothing to hold on to. I barely graduated from high school. The year following high school was almost entirely spent in front of a computer screen playing *World of Warcraft*. My diet consisted of Little Caesars Pizza and Mountain Dew. I had become the product of an environment I was internally conflicted with. But life had sent me on a rough ride and I was beginning to settle in, convincing myself that "this is just how life is."

Near the age of twenty, I decided to incrementally separate myself from my environment. This started by running a few times per week in the middle of the night by myself. My schedule didn't change much: sleeping and *World of Warcraft*. But those running stints throughout my week began to change me. Being outside the triggers and emotions of my environment allowed me to think clearly. I was able to think about the life I was creating for myself. I could see that I was adapting to a life I didn't want. I was able to think about who I wanted to be and the future and I wanted for myself.

After about six months of running, which culminated in a marathon in 2007, I made the decision to leave in January of 2008 just after my twentieth birthday. I needed out, a fresh start, a new beginning, a new identity. I knew I couldn't completely reset myself if I stayed home. I had tried attending community college and couldn't handle even a few classes. I ended up serving a church program on the opposite side of the country. I left my friends, family, consuming games, and even my inspiring runs.

A switch flipped.

In my new environment and role, I could be whoever I wanted to be. No one knew who I was. For two years, my entire mission consisted of unceasingly helping other people, often from far worse backgrounds than my own. In addition, I spent countless hours reading books and filling stacks of journals. My studies cemented my determination to one day become a writer.

When I returned home at twenty-two, I no longer fit my previous environment. I was different, and I was surprised by how much things had remained the same while I was gone. I threw myself into school, work, and reading as much as I could. With my newfound vision and skills, I breezed through my undergraduate work in three years, dated and married my wife, Lauren, and entered a prestigious PhD program in 2014 without submitting a formal application. During this time, I learned how to acquire quality mentors and maximize those relationships.

In January of 2015, four months after I began my PhD program, Lauren and I were approved as foster parents and took in a sibling group of three children, ages three, five, and seven. Becoming the parents of children from hard places has been a transformative experience for us all.

Although I had wanted to become a professional writer for over five years, my life was like a truck stuck in the snow. I couldn't get any traction to move forward. Becoming a foster parent was like filling the back of my truck with a load of wood. Once I had that weight of responsibility, I felt the immediate sense of urgency.

At the time, I was working a job on campus I hated to pay my tuition and provide for our family of five. The motivation created by my new situation as a father and provider gave me the courage to quit my university position to create time in my schedule to build my writing platform—a financial setback I believed to be a long-term investment in my career. I quit my job and began writing online in the spring of 2015.

I never had any doubts that I'd succeed as writer—not because of some inherent talent I possess but rather because my situation demands me to be successful. My wife and kids rely on me. Not only that, but I also see a great need in the world. Every person has enormous potential. If I can do anything to help other people, I will. The need is great.

I share my story as evidence that the principles in the book work. You can change. But you must change your environment. You must continually change your environment every time you're ready to upgrade yourself, which I hope becomes a pattern throughout your life. Never stop evolving. Never stop being transformed through experience and relationships, whether that be with others or even with your higher power.

You can do this.

Wherever you are, whatever you're dealing with, and whatever has happened to you, you can change. You can live your values and dreams. But it will never happen for you if you let your external world remain how it is. I can promise you that. I've watched most of the people in my life struggle to change because they've put all the pressure on themselves. It didn't work. It can't work.

When you change your environment, you will change. But

it must be *your choice*. If someone changes your environment for you, your chances of adapting long-term will be low. Although you are the product of your environment, that environment must be your proactive decision. Otherwise, you're living reactively.

Are you ready?

ACKNOWLEDGMENTS

This book would not be possible without the help of countless people. I'm grateful for all the help I've received from mentors, teachers, family, and friends. Specifically, I'm thankful to God for allowing me this brilliant life and for always being with me. I'm thankful to my wife, Lauren, for letting me live my dreams and for being my eternal companion. I'm thankful to our children, who challenge me every day to be a better person. I'm thankful to my mom and dad, Susan Knight and Phil Hardy, and my brothers, Trevor and Jacob, for providing me with inspiration and unconditional love. I'm thankful to my in-laws, Kay and Janae, for their love and financial support as I've built my writing career.

I'm thankful to Michelle Howry, my editor at Hachette, for finding my work on Medium.com, for giving me a chance, and for helping make this book what it is. I'm thankful to Ryan Holiday for the inspiring books he's written, for helping me write my book proposal and get my agent, and for helping me throughout the creation and marketing processes of this book. I'm thankful to Jimmy Soni for his editorial ideas and help on this book, for all the service he's given me for over two years, and for being a stand-up guy. I'm thankful to

Rachel Vogel, my agent, for helping me make smart career decisions and for her emotional support. I'm thankful to my graduate research adviser, Cindy Pury, for being patient and understanding. I know I was not a conventional nor ideal graduate student. I couldn't have asked for a better and more mindful graduate adviser. I'm thankful to Jeff Goins for his mentoring and friendship as I've built my writing career. I'm thankful to Richard Paul Evans for mentoring me in my writing, and in my life. I'm thankful to Joe Polish and the team at Genius Network for being incredibly generous and abundant toward my success. I'm thankful to Joel Weldon for how beautifully and powerfully he's helped me become a better speaker, and for his extreme generosity in providing me life-changing opportunities. I'm thankful to JR for helping me come up with the title for this book. You're a lifesaver!

I'm thankful to Nate Lambert for helping me develop my writing skills and for being one of my best friends ever since. I'm thankful to Jeffrey Reber and Brent Slife for what they taught me during my undergraduate education. They changed how I see everything, and much of this book is the product of what I learned from them. I'm thankful to Michael Barker, Jane Christensen, Brian Christensen, Matt Barlow, Steve Down, Wayne Beck, Alan and Linda Burns, Mirinda Call, and Richie Norton for being my support system and family. And to the many, many people I haven't mentioned specifically, thank you. I'm humbled and grateful. Finally, I'm thankful to all of the writers who have written books that have inspired me.

INDEX

ABOUT THE AUTHOR

Benjamin Hardy received his PhD in industrial and organizational psychology from Clemson University. Since late 2015, he's been the #1 writer on Medium.com, where he writes about self-improvement, motivation, and entrepreneurship. Benjamin's work is read by millions of people every month. He and his wife, Lauren, are the foster parents of three kids. They live in South Carolina.